Instructor's Manual to Accompany
SUPPES and WELLS:

THE **SOCIAL WORK** EXPERIENCE

AN INTRODUCTION TO THE PROFESSION

ANITA COWAN
Texas Woman's University

McGraw-Hill Publishing Company
New York St. Louis San Francisco Auckland Bogotá Caracas
Hamburg Lisbon London Madrid Mexico Milan
Montreal New Delhi Oklahoma City Paris San Juan
São Paulo Singapore Sydney Tokyo Toronto

This text was developed for McGraw-Hill
by Irving Rockwood & Associates, Inc.

Instructor's Manual to Accompany
Suppes and Wells:
THE SOCIAL WORK EXPERIENCE:
AN INTRODUCTION TO THE PROFESSION

ISBN 0-07-062608-1

234567890 GDP/GDP 9098765
Printer/Binder Greyden Press

CONTENTS

PREFACE

The material in this manual has been prepared to assist instructors who adopt Mary Ann Suppes' and Carolyn Wells' text, THE SOCIAL WORK EXPERIENCE: AN INTRODUCTION TO THE PROFESSION. This innovative introductory text uses extensive case applications to illustrate the diversity of settings and levels that characterize generalist practice.

Each chapter in this manual contains a chapter outline, a set of learning objectives (prepared by the authors of the text), a short list of additional readings, a set of class activities, and a set of test items. The latter are of four basic types: multiple-choice, true-false, fill-in, and essay. The essay questions in turn are divided (somewhat arbitrarily) into two basic types: short essay and essay. In all, the manual contains a total of 654 test items--205 multiple-choice, 197 true-false, 148 fill-in, and 104 essay questions. The average number of test items per chapter is 55. Of these, 17 are multiple-choice, 16 true-false, 12 fill-in, and 9 are essay. It should be noted here that the text itself also contains an extensive set of essay questions at the end of each chapter. These are of excellent quality and can readily be adapted for use as test questions or used as the basis for class activities.

As noted above, the manual also contains a set of exercises explicitly labeled as class activities. There are an average of just under 4 of these per chapter, a total of 44 in all. In general, my purpose in including these exercises is not to provide a definitive game plan for teaching from the text but rather to suggest some possible ways in which to do so. Ideally, these activities will stimulate further thinking about additional ways via which the instructor can reinforce or further explore the material provided in the text.

In preparing this manual I received encouragement and assistance from several quarters. I would especially like to thank the authors of THE SOCIAL WORK EXPERIENCE, Mary Ann Suppes and Carolyn Wells, for the display of confidence involved in inviting me to prepare this manual. In addition, I am grateful to Irv Rockwood of Irving Rockwood & Associates who contributed the test items for the last several chapters when circumstances made it impossible for me to do so.

Anita Cowan
Denton, Texas

CHAPTER 1. THE PROFESSIONAL SOCIAL WORKER

Chapter Outline

Susan Dunn (case study)
The Generalist Social Worker: Responsibilities and Roles
     Applying Competencies
     Interviewing--A Key Skill
     Exploring Options
Social Work and Related Professions
     Comparing Related Occupations
     How Professions Relate
Role of Professional Social Work Organizations
Baccalaureate Social Work Curriculum
     Human Diversity
     Research
     Values
     Code of Ethics

Learning Objectives

After reading Chapter 1, the student should be able to:

1. Define social work.

2. Identify ten competencies that a baccalaureate social worker should be able to perform.

3. Define generalist social work, and use the chapter case study to illustrate.

4. List the eight steps of the basic social work problem solving process.

5. Compare and contrast the profession of social work with the related fields of sociology, psychology, psychiatry, rehabilitation counseling, and urban affairs.

6. Identify the major professional social work organization in the United States concerned with social work practice issues.

7. List six major social work professional values.

8. List the six major categories of principles outlined in the NASW code of ethics.

9. Identify the major organization concerned with social work education in the United States.

10. Identify five major curriculum areas that a baccalaureate social work program must cover in order to be accredited by the CSWE.

11. Identify four major integrating themes required of baccalaureate social work programs by the CSWE.

Additional Reading Materials

Aquirre, B. E. "Why Do They Return? Abused Wives in Shelters." Social Work 30 (July-August 1985): 350-354.

Burden, D. S. and Gottlieb, N., "Battering and Abuse of Women in Intimate relationships," in D.S. Burden and N. Gottlieb, The Woman Client (New York: Tavistock Publications, 1987), pp. 209-22.

Federico, R. C. "Building on Our Strengths - The current State of Baccalaureate Education in Social Work." An occasional paper of the Association of Baccalaureate Program Directors. 1988.

Kremen, E., "The Social Work Profession Encounters the Battered Woman," in E. Norman and A. Mancuso, eds., Women's Issues and Social Work Practice (Itasca, IL: F.E. Peacock Publishers, Inc. 1980), pp. 113-132.

Walker, L. The Battered Woman Syndrome (New York: Springer, 1984).

Class Activities

1. To help illustrate the interaction between social worker and client during a conversation on a crisis telephone line, select two student volunteers to prepare and role play the dialogue on pages 1 through 6 of the textbook If possible, place a screen between the two students using a moveable chalk-board or other readily available prop, and supply each with a phone borrowed from a nearby office. (These need not actually be connected). In discussion following the role play, ask the class to identify the skills demonstrated by the social worker.

2. Invite a social worker from a local shelter to attend the class for a question and answer session on the use of the problem-solving process in domestic violence cases. Suggest a focus on the multiple roles of the social worker in this setting.

3. Form students into discussion groups for the purpose of exploring the dual focus on person and environment. Ask them to use the case study in the textbook and 1) discuss the problems of the client, Mrs. Dunn; 2) identify the systems with which she interacts; and 3) identify obstacles which require social work intervention. In class discussion following the exercise, list the group response to these issues on the chalkboard.

4. Provide each member of the class with an NASW student recruitment packet, and invite the local Unit Chairperson to make an appearance in the class. If possible, have the Chairperson make available for distribution to the class a handout on upcoming meetings and events.

Multiple-Choice

d)   1. The professional social worker who answered the crisis telephone line did all but which one of the following?
   a. clarified the purpose of the agency
   b. determined if the caller felt free to talk at that moment
   c. explored the nature of the client's immediate needs
   d. called the police while the client was on the line

c)   2. In assisting the caller, the social worker on the crisis line made the following decision:
   a. the caller needed to go directly to the hospital
   b. relatives were available to help the caller
   c. the caller sounded like someone the agency could help
   d. the caller would be able to afford the cost of the services

a)   3. The shelter for battered women in Chapter 1 had all but which one of the following features?
   a. a nurse on duty
   b. a secret address
   c. a playroom supervised by volunteers
   d. a private bedroom for each mother and child(ren)

d)   4. According to the definition in the text, social work is a profession concerned with the relationships between people and their environments. Such relationships affect the ability of people to do all but which one of the following:
   a. accomplish life tasks
   b. realize aspirations and values
   c. alleviate distress
   d. avoid cultural deprivation

b)   5. The generalist social worker is trained to provide all but which one of the following professional services?
   a. counseling with individuals and families
   b. psychotherapy
   c. working with groups
   d. identifying community resources

c)   6. Generalist social work can be defined in all but which one of the following ways:
   a. as a model designed to embrace the breadth of social work practice
   b. as a set of competencies in practice
   c. as a specialized method of behavior modification
   d. as the conscious use of an explicit problem-solving process

a)   7. For the social worker, problem-solving begins with:
   a. having advice on hand for the client
   b. gathering and assessing as much relevant data as possible
   c. a one-on-one interview
   d. reassuring the client that help is available

a)   8. In problem solving, the generalist social worker develops a plan of
action based upon which one of the following?
   a.   the nature of the particular problem
   b.   a method preferred by the social worker
   c.   the resources available within the agency
   d.   the primary client's view of the situation

c)   9. Accredited baccalaureate social work programs must include social work
practice and research as two of five major areas of instruction. Which one
of the following areas is not required?
   a.   research
   b.   field instruction
   c.   administration and management
   d.   social welfare policy and services

a)   10. Which one of the following statements is least likely to apply to the
typical BSW employed in an agency?
   a.   he or she is likely to be promoted to an administrative position.
   b.   his or her work is diverse and flexible.
   c.   he or she maintains a creative, problem-solving focus.
   d.   she or he intervenes at different levels of systems.

b)   11. Among the fields related to social work, which one of the following
emphasizes the social organization of groups?
   a.   psychology
   b.   sociology
   c.   psychiatry
   d.   urban affairs

c)   12. The social worker's dual focus on person and environment is sometimes
described as:
   a.   integrative
   b.   bimodal
   c.   ecological
   d.   sociological

b)   13. The basic functions of the National Association of Social Workers
(NASW) include all but which one of the following:
   a.   the establishment of professional standards
   b.   accreditation of schools and programs
   c.   membership services
   d.   professional action

a)   14. The National Association of Social Workers has provided a model
licensing law which provides for three levels of practice. Which of the
following is not one of the levels included in this model?
   a.   caseworker
   b.   certified social worker
   c.   social worker
   d.   associate

b)   15. Among the integrative themes in the social work curriculum, which one is <u>not</u> necessarily found in all required courses?
   a. human diversity
   b. democratic action
   c. values and ethics
   d. research

True-False

T   1. The social worker who took the call at the women's shelter had an undergraduate professional education in social work.

F   2. A generalist social worker at the baccalaureate level is a specialist in psychotherapy with individuals or families.

T   3. The accrediting body for professional social work programs is the Council on Social Work Education.

T   4. The problem-solving skills which a BSW should be able to demonstrate were described by Baer and Federico as 10 competencies.

F   5. In social work terminology, the person who brings a problem is known as a "patient".

F   6. A social worker will gather relevant data on a problem situation only from the person who initiates a request for assistance.

T   7. The problem-solving process used by a professionally educated social worker involves a specific sequence of steps.

T   8. Social workers employed in shelters for battered women are primarily engaged in problem-solving at the individual and family levels.

T   9. Data gathering may require obtaining signed permissions.

T   10. The best plans for action are made only after options have been identified and explored.

T   11. Decisions concerning the action taken in response to a problem are ultimately made by the social worker.

T   12. The process of agreeing upon a plan of action is known as "contracting".

F   13. The social work contract always takes the form of a written agreement.

T   14. The professional social work education curriculum as established by the CSWE presumes a basic liberal arts foundation including courses in both the social and biological sciences.

T   15. Graduate education in social work typically provides specialized training in working with differing sizes of social systems.

F 16. A social worker will use knowledge from sociology much more than that from psychology in day-to-day practice.

T 17. BSWs are eligible for full membership in NASW.

T 18. Legal regulation of social workers (i.e. licensure) helps protect consumers by ensuring that someone who has the title of social worker is a fully trained professional.

T 19. Human diversity factors will strongly influence the kinds of intervention plans acceptable to a given client.

F 20. Social workers follow a formalized Code of Ethics but have not explicitly identified a set of values for the profession.

Fill-In

1. The baccalaureate social worker learns the skills to be a (generalist) practitioner.

2. The national accrediting body for professional social work programs is the (Council on Social Work Education).

3. The basic steps of the problem solving process are: (gathering information from all relevant sources; assessing information; defining the problem; planning for action; developing an explicit contract for action; carrying out the action plan; evaluating results; and terminating when appropriate).

4. A basic skill employed by professional social workers to obtain information from clients and others is (interviewing).

5. The discipline which emphasizes the study of the mind and behavior is (psychology).

6. Baccalaureate social work students are required to take courses in social and biological sciences to assist development of a(n) (ecological) perspective.

7. Besides diverse ethnic and cultural groups, people differ according to: (age, gender, physical health, mental abilities, lifestyle, and sexual preference).

8. Values are (beliefs); ethics are (behaviors) prescribed by values.

Short Essay

1. Define social work as a profession.

2. Describe a minimum of four needs that a client in a shelter for battered women is likely to have.

3. Describe the difference between sociology and social work.

4. Describe the specific services provided by NASW to its membership.

5. Describe some of the types of things social workers may learn through conducting research.

Essay

1. Write an essay identifying, describing, and explaining the competencies required of a generalist social worker.

2. Write an essay identifying the diverse skills required of a social worker in a shelter for battered women and describe the way in which each would be used at multiple levels of the problem-solving process.

3. Write an essay describing and defending the major values of the social work profession.

CHAPTER 2. SOCIAL WORK'S USE OF SOCIAL WELFARE RESOURCES

Chapter Outline

The Schultz Family (case study)
Income Maintenance and the Institution of Social Welfare
    Social Welfare Concepts
    Old World Historical Roots
    The Elizabethan Poor Law and the Act of Settlement
    New Concepts in Poor Law
Poor Relief in the United States
    Values
    Charity Organization Society and the Settlement House Movement
Social Legislation in the Twentieth Century
    The Progressive Years, 1900-1930
    Federal Initiatives, 1930-1968
    Cutting Back the Welfare State, 1968-Present
Issues and Concerns in Income Maintenance
    Research Related to Public Welfare
    Issues for the Future
    Social Work Roles in Income Maintenance
Summary

Learning Objectives

After Reading Chapter 2, the student should be able to:

1. Define social welfare, and describe how it relates to social work.

2. Compare and contrast the institutional and residual concepts of social welfare.

3. Define income maintenance and describe four examples of federally financed income maintenance programs as illustrated in the case study.

4. Define means test.

5. Describe the categories into which poor people were divided according to the Elizabethan Poor Law of 1601, and list the provisions made for each category.

6. Identify the innovations in poor law made by the Speenhamland Act, and discuss why this act eventually was repealed.

7. Discuss different value systems held by members of the Charity Organization Society and the Settlement Movement, and how they led to different interventive strategies.

8. Describe three types of federal provisions originally made available under the Social Security Act, and their funding.

9. Identify at least six programs intended to alleviate poverty that were implemented during the War on Poverty years.

10. Discuss the apparent political agenda of the 1980s with respect to welfare programs for poor people.

11. Identify at least four groups of people who are particularly vulnerable to poverty and explain why.

12. Discuss the role of research in examining common myths about the AFDC program.

Additional Reading Materials

Block, F., Cloward, R. A., Ehrenreich, B., and Piven, F. F. The Mean Season: The Attack on the Welfare State (New York: Pantheon Books, 1987).

Day, P. J. A New History of Social Welfare (Englewood Cliffs, NJ: Prentice-Hall, 1989).

How the Poor Would Remedy Poverty (Washington, DC: Coalition on Human Needs, 1988).

Danziger, S. H. and Weisburg, D. H., eds. Fighting Poverty (Cambridge, MA: Harvard University Press, 1986).

Dudley, W., ed. Opposing Viewpoints-Poverty (St. Paul, MN: Greenhaven Press).

Hefferman, J., Shuttlesworth, G., and Ambrosino, R., "The Fight Against Poverty" in J. Hefferman, G. Shuttlesworth, and R. Ambrosino, Social Work and Social Welfare (St. Paul, MN: West Publishing Company), pp. 65-92.

Folbre, N. A Field Guide to the U.S. Economy (New York: Pantheon Books, 1987).

Jansson, B. The Reluctant Welfare State (New York: Columbia University Press, 1988).

Segal, E. A. "Welfare Reform: Help for Women and Children?" Affilia 4 (Fall 1989): 42-50.

"Special Issue on Social Welfare, Social Insurance and Social Security," Social Work 34 (July 1989).

Class Activities

1. Have students bring to class current newspaper and magazine articles on poverty in American and welfare programs, and allow time for them to report on their articles and organize these on posters or a bulletin board. Encourage them to identify the residual or institutional views expressed in newspaper editorials. Recommend that they supplement their reading by watching news programs such as Washington Week in Review on public television.

2. Have the students form into small groups. Ask each group to identify three examples of the way in which their efforts to achieve a college education have been reinforced by their values. Then ask them to reflect on the values which have led them to choose studies in social work.

3. Divide the students into small groups and provide each group with a) a brief written portrait of a family consisting of a mother with two small children, and b) an AFDC application from the local welfare office. Have students fill out the application to the extent possible. Have one student from each group report to the class on "barriers" encountered in the application.

4. Invite a speaker from the local AFDC office to speak to the class on current welfare programs in the community. This can be particularly useful if the speaker can be prepared to discuss the ways in which current reform legislation is being implemented.

5. Prepare a role play with three students taking the role of AFDC recipients and three students taking the role of conservative politicians who are seeking to curb benefits. Have each side prepare their basic perspectives from the standpoint of institutional versus residual approaches to social welfare. Allow each side time to state their position and then follow with questions. The instructor may serve as moderator for the dialogue.

TEST ITEMS

Multiple-Choice

c) 1. In Chapter 2, Ms. Lydia Schultz and her daughter, Myra, became known to Jewish Family Services as a result of:
a. a call from Myra's teacher at school
b. an outreach program established by the agency
c. a referral from Ms. Schultz's social worker at a sheltered workshop
d. a referral from the city housing department

a) 2. The social worker from Jewish Family Services learned that most of Ms. Schultz's income was derived from several government programs. Which one of the following programs did not provide financial support to the family?
a. Workman's Compensation
b. Supplemental Security Income (SSI)
c. Aid to Families with Dependent Children (AFDC)
d. Food Stamps

d) 3. As the nature of the problems experienced by Ms. Schultz and daughter Myra were explored by the social worker, it seemed that the primary "problem for work" was:
a. Ms. Schultz' lack of formal education
b. the poor relationship between mother and daughter
c. the need for adequate housing for the family
d. Myra's frustration with academic performance at the public school

b)   4. A social worker had been designated as "payee" for Ms. Schultz' monthly income because:
  a. Ms. Schultz was physically disabled and unable to go to the bank
  b. Ms. Schultz was mentally retarded
  c. The Schultz family lived in a high-crime neighborhood
  d. Ms. Schultz had failed to report over-payments

a)   5. Income maintenance has been defined in the text as having <u>all but which one</u> of the following characteristics?
  a. it is payable for a limited period of time
  b. it is a field of social welfare
  c. it is provided during periods of income interruption or reduction
  d. it is provided to both individuals and families

b)   6. The concept of "residual" social welfare includes <u>all but which one</u> of the following viewpoints?
  a. people should normally be able to meet all their needs through their own family
  b. there should be no formalized welfare services in society
  c. the welfare system gets involved only as an emergency measure
  d. services are accompanied by the stigma of charity

d)   7. The "institutional" concept of social welfare is based on the belief that:
  a. formal assistance should be available after there are problems
  b. social welfare services are earmarked for those without families
  c. institutions will need more assistance than individuals and families
  d. social welfare services are normal, first-line functions of modern industrial society

c)   8. When considering the Old World historical roots of social welfare systems, which one of the following did <u>not</u> have an influence on later development?
  a. reciprocal helping roles in small-scale societies
  b. alms-giving through religious groups
  c. the increase in feudal societies throughout Europe
  d. the 1349 Statute of Laborers in England

b)   9. The Elizabethan Poor Law of 1601 offered aid to those considered "deserving" of assistance. Which of the following qualified?
  a. able-bodied adults who were homeless
  b. old, disabled persons and dependent children
  c. any widow with more than three children
  d. impoverished relatives of the clergy

c)   10. Which of the following is <u>not</u> one of the acts that made important changes in the poor law of England?
  a. Settlement Act of 1662
  b. Speenhamland Act of 1795
  c. Patriot Relief Act of 1812
  d. New Poor Law of 1834

a) 11. After the American Revolution, relief of the poor became a prerogative of:
a. state government
b. federal government
c. local church councils
d. county agencies

b) 12. In The Wealth of Nations, Adam Smith in 1776 argues in favor of the principle of:
a. manifest destiny
b. laissez-faire
c. selective taxation
d. social paternalism

c) 13. The social philosopher, Herbert Spencer, argued that:
a. taxation created dependency among the poor
b. poor relief contributed to overpopulation
c. only the fittest people should survive
d. the human race could not survive without cooperation among people

c) 14. Early methods of organization, investigation and written records, which proved to be useful in social welfare work, were developed by:
a. The Red Cross
b. settlement houses
c. Charity Organization Society
d. Freedmen's Bureau

d) 15. The settlement house movement was an early manifestation of:
a. the residual approach to social welfare
b. the evangelical mission of churches
c. newly-obtained federal support of social agencies
d. the institutional approach to welfare services

b) 16. The workmen's compensation laws that were passed during the early 1900s reflected the belief that:
a. men seeking work should receive assistance
b. people deserve assistance in the case of industrial accidents
c. workers should be compensated when they retire
d. unions should have a voice in determining pay scales of workers

a) 17. Which one of the following was not established by the Social Security Act of 1935?
a. homestead protection
b. social insurance
c. public assistance
d. health and welfare services

c) 18. The period of greatest progress in securing passage of legislation reflecting an institutional view of social welfare services was:
a. 1880-1900
b. 1900-1930
c. 1930-1968
d. 1968-present

b)   19. The purpose of the welfare bill passed in the closing days of the Reagan
administration (December 1988) was to:
a. allow unemployed mothers to remain at home with their children
b. drive AFDC adult beneficiaries off welfare and into the job market
c. increase benefit levels for mothers and children
d. insure salaries greater than minimum wage for those getting off welfare

True-False

T   1.   More than half of AFDC recipients remain on the program for less than
three years.

F   2.   Social work is unique in that it is the only profession to take an
active interest in social welfare issues.

T   3.   Under the Elizabethan Poor Law, aid provided to persons in their own
homes was known as "outdoor relief."

F   4.   The federal government was involved in programs of relief to the poor by
1800.

T   5.   Former slaves were the first persons to benefit from welfare assistance
funded by federal tax dollars.

T   6.   Mutual aid and self-help were the primary concepts involved in the
settlement house movement.

F   7.   Jane Addams established Hull House before the beginning of the Industrial Revolution.

T   8.   Both Community Organization Society and settlement house workers were
active as advocates for social legislation in the early 1900s.

T   9.   The Children's Bureau, established in 1909, provided national leadership
in protective legislation.

F   10. The stigma of charity is attached to both social insurance and public
assistance.

F   11. General assistance programs are available to the poor in all states of
the nation.

T   12. AFDC was not included when Supplemental Security Income was established
in 1974.

T   13. The Work Incentive (WIN) Program was not successful in cutting costs
and reducing welfare roles.

F   14. The United States is a leader among industrialized nations in providing
free health care to its citizens.

T   15. Research has shown that receiving welfare benefits does not result in
recipients having large numbers of children.

Fill-In

1. Social welfare is a nation's (system) of programs, benefits, and services that help meet the human needs that are fundamental to society.

2. (England) is the country that provided the model for early social welfare programs in America.

3. The belief that the condition of a poor person who receives "relief" should be worse than the poorest laborer in the community gave rise to the principles of (lesser eligibility).

4. The first federal agency to use public tax monies to assist the poor was the (Freedmen's Bureau).

5. The principal form of help offered by the Charity Organization Society was "(moral uplift)."

6. Perhaps the best-known leader of the Charity Organization Society was (Mary Richmond).

7. At the time of passage of the Social Security Act, the President of the United States was (Franklin D. Roosevelt).

8. The book by Michael Harrington that stimulated the federal government's War on Poverty was titled (The Other America).

9. The best-known example of federal vouchers available to people of low income is (food stamps).

10. Evaluating a client's financial resources and using the result to determine eligibility to receive a benefit is (means testing).

11. According to current "welfare reform" legislation, persons getting off of AFDC and becoming employed will receive time-limited assistance with (child care) and (health care).

Short Essay

1. Briefly describe the type of assistance provided to Ms. Schultz and her daughter, Myra, by the social worker with Jewish Family Services.

2. Describe the intent and function of the first Elizabethan Poor Law.

3. Describe the areas of service provided by the first settlement houses.

4. Describe one of the "myths" about people who receive social welfare and provide evidence that corrects the myth.

<u>Essay</u>

1. Describe the relationship between social work and social welfare.

2. Both residual and institutional approaches influence the nature of our social welfare system today. Compare and contrast these two approaches and provide examples which illustrate the influence of each on current social welfare programs.

3. Identify and discuss the values that have shaped the social welfare system. Discuss conflicts which exist between these values.

4. Discuss reasons for increases in poverty among: a) children; b) women; and c) the elderly during the past decade.

CHAPTER 3. SOCIAL WORK IN HEALTH CARE

Chapter Outline

Katherine Lewandowski (case study)
The Knowledge and Skill Base of Practice
    Values and Ethics
    Human Diversity and the Community
    Continuing Professional Development: A Responsibility
The Growth of Social Work in Health Care
    The Health Care Legacy
    Medical Social Work in the United States
    Regional Differences in Health Care Social Work
    Changing Roles of the Social Worker in Health Care
Other Illustrations of Social Work Practice in Health Care
Public Policy: Its Impact on Patients, Providers, and Practice
    Medicare
    Medicaid
    The Evolution of Health Care Financing in the United States
    Current Issues
Summary

Learning Objectives

After reading Chapter 3, the student should be able to:

1. Discuss the learning that took place for the student social worker in her field placement at St. Anne's Hospital.

2. Identify the required and elective liberal arts courses that help to prepare social work students for practice in health care.

3. Describe several significant events in the history of health care social work; identify at least two persons who provided leadership or direction and explain the nature of their contribution to this field of practice.

4. Provide three characteristics of health care in rural America that differentiate it from health care in larger metropolitan areas.

5. Give an example to demonstrate blurring of boundaries between health care professionals.

6. Explain why discharge planning is an important role for hospital social workers.

7. Define "ataque" and explain the circumstance which are likely to precipitate it.

8. List five social or psychological problems that HMO social workers are likely to work with.

9. Differentiate Medicaid from Medicare; explain the major provisions of each program.

10. Define DRGs and explain the positive and also the potentially negative outcomes of such programs.

11. Discuss the concept of national health insurance and universal coverage of health care.

Additional Reading Materials

Abramson, J. S. "Participation of Elderly Patients in Discharge Planning: Is Self-Determination a Reality?" Social Work 33 (1988): 443-448.

Berkman, B., Kember, B., Marcus, L., and Silberman, P. "Course Content for Social Work Practice in Health Care," Journal of Social Work Education 21 (1985): 43-51.

Gordon, M. S. "Social Work Practice in Health Care: Some Ethical Considerations," in S. Dillick, ed., Value Foundations of Social Work (Detroit, MI: School of Social Work, Wayne State University, 1984).

"Special Issue on Hospital Social Work," Health and Social Work 15 (February, 1990).

Holden, M. O. "Meeting Diagnostic Related Group Goals for Elderly Patients," Health and Social Work 14 (1989): 13-21.

Kerson, T. S. Social Work in Health Settings: Practice in Context 2nd ed. (New York: Haworth Press, 1989).

NASW Commission on Health and Mental Health. Making Our Case: A Resource Book of Selected Materials for Social Workers in Health Care (Silver Spring, MD: National Association of Social Workers, 1989).

Siefert, K. "The Generalist's Role," in L. Henk, ed., Social Work and Primary Care (Beverly Hills, CA: Sage Publications), pp. 55-66.

Class Activities

1. An activity such as the following can be a stimulating way to introduce the field of health care and highlight issues related to health and illness. Bring a portable cassette player to class and provide students with manila paper and magic markers. Ask them to draw a picture that captures their idea of good health. Allow ten minutes for this exercise, and play a recording of bright, lively music during the time allotted. Then repeat the exercise, only this time play melancholy background music and have the students draw a picture representing illness. When their drawings are completed, ask students to share the pictures and their thoughts with the class.

2. In order to reinforce learning about the practice of social work in health care, have the students form three groups--A, B, and C. Ask group A to generate a list of values; group B to generate a list of types of knowledge; and group C to list important skills needed for social work practice in health care settings. Ask each group to designate two group members to report back to the class. Lists can be put on chalkboard or newsprint pads.

3. Ask students to form task groups to compare and contrast actual and proposed health coverage programs. Assign each group one of the following topics to investigate and discuss: a) Medicare, b) Medicaid, c) the Kennedy-Waxman bill, and d) the Health Partnership Security proposal. Provide each group with a brief list of newspaper articles from sources such as The New York Times and NASW News to supplement the information provided in the textbook. Ask each group to prepare a brief, oral report for the following class period.

4. Guest speakers often bring informative and interesting insights on the local health care system into the classroom. While time will not permit using all of the following, consider inviting one or more of these to speak to your class: a) a social worker from the community hospital; b) a social worker from a nursing home; c) a social worker from a hospice program; or d) a pair of social workers--one from a non-profit public hospital and one from a hospital operated by a health care corporation.

5. Social work classes are often composed of students from diverse cultural backgrounds. If this is true of your class, ask for volunteers to share on a panel presentation of health care in their families and communities of origin. These discussions are helpful in expanding students' awareness of differential diagnosis and treatment apart from those utilized by the medical community.

TEST ITEMS

Multiple-Choice

b) 1. The case study on social work in health care featured a social worker who was:
    a. an advanced clinical practitioner
    b. a baccalaureate social work student in field placement
    c. a masters level social work student in field placement
    d. a post-masters social work unit administrator

a) 2. The health care setting described in the case was a:
    a. community general hospital
    b. nursing home
    c. rehabilitation center
    d. hospice

b) 3. In the case study, the social worker had concerns related to her assigned responsibilities in:
    a. establishing a contract with the patient
    b. assisting with discharge planning for the patient
    c. preparing the family for the patient's surgery

d) 4. In the case study, the social worker prepared to raise questions based on her concerns because:
a. a number of patients shared complaints to her
b. admissions criteria had become more rigid
c. the social work staff was unaware of the problem
d. a number of former patients had recently died

c) 5. As work was planned for evaluation of the policy under consideration in the case study, which one of the following was not a part of planning?
a. research would be needed to collect data on the perceived problem
b. lines of authority within the institution would have to be followed
c. publicity through the media would need to be generated
d. federal guidelines would have to be considered

a) 6. Generalist social workers in hospitals generally have all but which one of the following responsibilities?
a. engaging in long term counseling with individuals and their families
b. working with support groups for patients who have a health problem in common
c. referring patients and their families to appropriate community resources
d. collaborating with other professionals on staff

d) 7. Current requirements in the Curriculum Policy Statement of the Accreditation Commission of the Council on Social Work Education underscore the importance of providing content in all but which one of the following areas:
a. values and ethics
b. oppression and discrimination
c. human diversity
d. economic theory

c) 8. The English forerunners of today's health care social workers were known as:
a. friendly visitors
b. medical caseworkers
c. lady almoners
d. parish health watchmen

b) 9. The person who is generally considered the originator of medical social work in the United States is:
a. Clara Barton
b. Ida Cannon
c. Dorothea Dix
d. Lillian Wald

c) 10. The first hospital social service department in the United States was developed in:
a. Wisconsin
b. New York
c. Massachusetts
d. Delaware

19

a) 11. The social worker in a rural health care facility will:
a. have considerable community involvement
b. have support from other social workers in similar settings in the area
c. have to be less creative in developing resources
d. have to use specialized, rather than generalist, practice skills

d) 12. As people experience large gaps in health care resources, all but which one of the following are contributing factors?
a. lack of access to facilities from rural areas
b. lack of hospitalization insurance
c. too many assets to qualify for federal assistance
d. too much money being spent on research and not enough on treatment

b) 13. According to data gathered by the American Hospital Association, the percentage of hospital social workers involved with discharge planning is:
a. 65
b. 94
c. 37
d. 100

b) 14. Among new trends in health care delivery is a system which usually contracts with employers to provide employee "members" health care for a fee. This is known as a:
a. Diagnostic Related Group Insurance
b. Health Maintenance Organization
c. Supplemental Health Corporation
d. Medial Services Union

c) 15. The recent implementation of cost containment procedures in hospitals has resulted in:
a. overall reduction in health-related expenses for the federal government
b. reduction of acutely ill patients in nursing homes
c. increase in discharge of patients who have continuing health needs
d. increased recovery rates among patients during hospitalization

a) 16. Medicare was established by the federal government in 1966 to provide health care payments for:
a. persons 65 and older and for long term disabled persons
b. persons of all ages who are poor
c. persons of all ages who are covered by Social Security
d. persons 65 and older who have less than $10,000 of health insurance

d) 17. Medicaid differs from Medicare in that it is a program that:
a. covers the "old old" in society
b. was established many years before Medicare
c. covers only hospitalization expenses
d. requires a "means test" for eligibility

c) 18. Both Medicare and Medicaid continue to be at the forefront of health policy debates because:
a. neither program covers poor children
b. Social Security can no longer maintain both programs
c. costs of the programs have increased substantially
d. they are time limited programs scheduled to expire in 1995

b)   19. In a study of New Jersey's four-year experience with cost containment procedures, it was found that hospital social work departments were:
a. having less impact on patient care
b. in a position to strengthen their roles
c. experiencing reduced patient case loads
d. deferring more to the authority of physicians

b)   20. In 1989, the National Association of Social Workers joined a coalition that was proposing a national health plan known as the:
a. Basic Health Benefits for All Americans Act
b. Health Security Partnership
c. Catastrophic Coverage Act
d. Family Health Maintenance Initiative

True-False

T   1. The student in the case study, Linda Sanders, was in her senior year of social work field placement.

F   2. The student felt more secure among the health care professionals when she wore the white lab coat used by the social work staff.

T   3. Kathryn Lewandowski, the patient, had been admitted to the facility for surgery to repair a fractured hip.

T   4. Linda Sanders became concerned about her patient when Ms. Lewandowski appeared withdrawn and in distress.

F   5. Linda Sanders was able to make a follow-up visit with Ms. Lewandowski a month after the patient's surgery.

T   6. Linda Sanders' preparation for generalist social work practice included courses in both social policy and practice methods.

F   7. As part of her assignments, Linda Sanders was to have responsibility for directing efforts to re-evaluate institutional policy.

T   8. Learning to make appropriate referrals to local social service agencies and other programs was among the opportunities available to Linda Sanders.

T   9. Coursework in baccalaureate social work programs provides a basic understanding of biological sciences.

T   10. The generalist social worker is prepared to intervene with small and large groups, as well as with individuals and families.

T   11. Baccalaureate social work students begin their preparation for generalist practice with a foundation of liberal arts courses.

T   12. Health care social workers routinely encounter ethical dilemmas in daily practice.

F   13. The knowledge of community that a health care social worker is expected to have will be limited to lists of available resources.

T   14. One of the first types of early European health are facilities was that which provided care for avalanche victims.

T   15. Health care social workers were the first to establish a professional organization.

F   16. Lack of health care resources is a condition unique to rural settings.

T   17. Facilities owned by private health are corporations generally do not extend services beyond those covered by health insurance.

T   18. For the past decade, the leading advocate in the U.S. Senate for a national health plan has been Edward Kennedy.

Fill-In

1. When social work student, Linda Sanders, needed to review concerns and clarify procedures surrounding Ms. Lewandowski's situation, she did this with her (field instructor).

2. The minimum number of hours of field education for baccalaureate social work students is (400).

3. The policy that Linda Sanders was acutely concerned about was that of (discharge planning).

4. The health care social worker is the essential link between the patient, the health care facility, and (the community).

5. Two recent, increasing health problems that are requiring ongoing learning for even experienced social workers are (AIDS) and (babies born to cocaine-addicted mothers).

6. In 1955, the American Association of Medial Social Workers merged with other independent social work organizations to become the (National Association of Social Workers).

7. The majority of health care social workers today are employed by (hospitals).

8. The health care program which specializes in providing care for terminally ill persons is known as a (hospice).

9. The decline of energy for or interest in one's profession is commonly known as (burn-out).

10. In a case example illustrating cultural diversity, a young Puerto Rican mother in distress had a type of seizure known in Spanish as an (ataque).

11. Persons who lack insurance coverage or other financial resources to cover the cost of treatment and follow-up care are identified as (medically indigent).

12. The best example of a health care setting which calls for fast-paced crises intervention work and brief contact with clients is the (hospital emergency room).

13. The provision of Medicare that is voluntary and that extends service beyond basic coverage is known as (Part B).

14. The medical insurance program that is financed by a federal tax deduction from an employee's paycheck if (Medicare, Part A).

15. The one state that does not participate in Medicaid is (Arizona).

16. The majority of Medicaid recipients are members of families who receive (AFDC).

17. The majority of Medicaid expense provide health care for (the elderly) and (the disabled).

18. In 1983, the federal government instituted a hospital payment program which came to be known as the (Diagnostic Related Group) plan.

19. According to a quotation cited in the text, the only other industrial country (beside the U.S.) in the world to tolerate a system in which a family's health is determined by a family's wealth is (South Africa).

Short Essay

1. Briefly describe why the patient in the case study was transferred from one health care setting to another several days after surgery.

2. Define the term "ethical dilemma" and provide an example of one which social workers encounter in health care settings.

3. Describe three resources available to practicing social workers for continuing professional education.

4. Provide two reasons why the American Medical Association has consistently opposed national health insurance.

Essay

1. From the discussion of the events in the case study on health care, discuss what the nursing home social worker might have done to possibly prevent the death of Katherine Lewandowski.

2. Describe the knowledge, values, and skills that a generalist social worker would need in a health care setting.

3. Compare and contrast the federal programs of Medicare and Medicaid.

4. Describe the health care financing system that currently exists in our country. What advantages and disadvantages would there be if a national health insurance plan were adopted?

5. Discuss the discharge planning responsibilities of social workers in health care systems including the seven social work roles published by the American Hospital Association in 1985.

CHAPTER 4. FAMILY AND CHILDREN'S SERVICES

Chapter Outline

Latitia Phillips (case study)
Services and Their Providers
    In-Home Services
    Out-of-Home Substitute Services
Client Self-Determination and Professional Decision Making
Historical Perspective on Family and Children's Services
    Protective Services
    Notion of Children's Rights
    Social Work with Families
Family Policy: Research Raises Questions
Summary

Learning Objectives

After reading Chapter 4, the student should be able to:

1. Discuss the purpose of "in-home" services.

2. Identify seven major "in-home" services for children and families.

3. Identify five major "out-of-home" substitute services for children and families.

4. Discuss the social work value of self-determination, and how it can be adapted in situations of working with minor children.

5. Discuss the first court case to protect a minor child.

6. Identify the Title of the Social Security Act and the date in which protective services were finally mandated by federal law.

7. Describe how sexism and classicism may have eclipsed social work's early focus on the family.

8. Discuss research findings regarding incidence of poverty among American children today.

9. Discuss effects of poverty on family stability.

10. Discuss the principal purpose of the 1989 Moynihan welfare reform bill, and its likely, if unintended, consequences.

Additional Reading Materials

Barbarino, J., Schellenback, J., and Sibes, J. Troubled Youth, Troubled Families (Hawthorne, NY: Aldine de Gruyter, 1986).

Costin, L. B. and Rapp, C. A. _Child Welfare Policies and Practice_ 2nd ed. (New York: McGraw-Hill, 1984).

Knitzer, J. "Children's Rights in the Family and Society: Dilemmas and Realities," _American Journal of Orthopsychiatry_ 52 (1982): 481-495.

Gonzalez-Santeen, E. and Learn, A., eds. _Collaboration the Key: A Model Curriculum on Indian Child Welfare_ (Tempe, AZ: School of Social Work, Arizona State University, 1989).

McGowan, B. G. and Meegan, W., eds. _Child Welfare: Current Dilemmas and Future Directions_ (Itasca, IL: F. E. Peacock Publisher, Inc, 1983).

Skaff, L. F. "Child Maltreatment Coordinating Committees for Effective Service Delivery," _Child Welfare_ 69 (1988).

A Social Worker's Guide to the Family Support Act of 1988 (Silver Spring, MD: National Association of Social Workers, 1989).

"Special Issue on Public Child Welfare and Family Issues," _Social Work_ 33 (November-December 1988).

"Special Issue on Strengthening Families," _Social Work_ 35 (May 1990).

Class Activities

1. To better explore the feelings and actions in the Latitia Phillips case, ask for volunteers to describe what is taking place from the point of view of each of the following persons: a) Latitia Phillips; b) Betty Phillips; c) Mr. Taylor; d) Aunt LaVrene; e) Danielle Rose; and f) George Petit. Allow each student 5-7 minutes to make their presentation. Students taking the part of one of the family members should be encouraged to express their feelings, both positive and negative. The family therapist should attempt to describe the issues and emotions raised during the brief period of family therapy. Have the protective services worker introduce and close the presentation with an overview of his work. This assignment should be made one class session prior to the exercise to allow students to prepare their presentations.

2. As an alternate exercise for studying the Phillips case, have the class form into task groups and provide each group with sheets of newsprint and magic markers. Have each group draw a "road map" of the social work action process followed by the protective services worker. (Students will need their books.) Students may find it helpful to devise a set of symbols to represent events or actions such as family conflict, runaway behavior, court action, etc. Have each group show and explain their drawing to the class. While the maps will vary, each should begin with the intake worker receiving a call from the police.

3. This exercise is useful but depends on the availability of multiple copies of local resource guides. If such guides are available, have the students form two task groups--one representing in-home services and the other out-of-home services. Using the guides, have each group prepare a list of local resources that fit their category with examples, where found, of specific

local services. To ensure uniformity, provide each group with formatted 8 1/2 x 11 sheets of paper for recording their information. If desired, produce overhead transparencies from the information sheets and use them to make a visual presentation of each group's findings during the following class period. You may wish to have a member of each group provide a general description of his or her group's category of services by way of introduction. This exercise will also point up where services are non-existent.

TEST ITEMS

Multiple-Choice

b) 1. Eleven year old Latitia Phillips had spent her childhood living with her:
a. grandmother
b. father, mother, and older siblings
c. mother and younger siblings
d. father and step mother

c) 2. After her father's death, and the loss of his earnings to the family, Latitia qualified for and received financial support from:
a. Aid to Families with Dependent Children (AFDC)
b. General Assistance funds
c. Social Security Survivor's Benefits
d. Child Support payments

c) 3. Latitia began to have real difficulty when she was living with:
a. her mother and grandmother
b. her older brother
c. her mother and Mr. Taylor
d. her aunt and uncle

a) 4. The protective services unit of the County Department of Social Services became involved with Latitia following:
a. a call from the police
b. a complaint from neighbors
c. a referral from Latitia's teacher
d. a request for help from Latitia's mother

c) 5. When George Petit, the protective services worker, began his investigation, he discovered all but which one of the following:
a. Latitia's mother wanted Latitia to be returned to her immediately
b. there was a report of physical abuse
c. there was a report of sexual abuse
d. Latitia was herself requesting protection

a) 6. Throughout the assessment phase, the social worker, George Petit, kept in mind the overall aim of protective services work which is to:
a. restore the security of the child's own home
b. expose the perpetrators of child abuse
c. allow children the right of self-determination
d. terminate parental custody when child abuse is suspected

26

d) 7. During the course of Latitia's case, court orders were utilized for all but which one of the following:
    a. the transfer of Latitia's custody from her mother to the county
    b. the mandatory provision of family counseling
    c. the placement of Latitia in a group home
    d. a psychological evaluation of Latitia

a) 8. Professional social workers employed in the field of children and family services experience all but which one of the following:
    a. increasing demand for persons with their skills and training
    b. a high degree of job satisfaction
    c. high levels of job-related stress
    d. extensive opportunities to apply generalist social work knowledge and skills in day-to-day practice

c) 9. "In-home" services are those which:
    a. are always offered in the client's actual home
    b. provide all forms of "home and shelter"
    c. support the family's ability to live together
    d. specialize in adoption and foster care

a) 10. Today quite a few people seeking to adopt children try to do so privately through an attorney because:
    a. there are waiting lists for normal babies at social agencies
    b. they do not have to go through a home study
    c. it is less expensive
    d. they obtain greater protection of their legal rights as parents

d) 11. One drawback of runaway youth shelters from the point of view of the children involved is:
    a. discharge always requires a hearing in Children's Court
    b. the goal of crisis counseling provided through the shelter is to arrange for placement in long-term foster care
    c. they must be interviewed by a protective services worker from the county
    d. their families must consent for them to stay in the shelter

b) 12. Which of the following provides the most restrictive environment?
    a. a runaway shelter
    b. residential treatment
    c. a group home
    d. foster care

a) 13. In the 1870s, the case of a badly abused child, Mary Ellen, was taken to court by the:
    a. Society for Prevention of Cruelty to Animals (SPCA)
    b. Society for Prevention of Cruelty to Children (SPCC)
    c. Charity Organization Society
    d. New York Foundling Hospital

c) 14. According to a survey of family service agencies, the major family-related problems currently include all but which one of the following:
    a. single parenthood
    b. unemployment
    c. lack of choice in family planning
    d. alcohol and drug abuse

<u>True-False</u>

T. 1. Latitia's financial assistance was to stop when she turned 18.

F. 2. The crisis in Latitia's home life occurred when one of the adults became a cocaine addict.

T. 3. The protective services social worker, George Petit, was aware of the strength of black families.

F. 4. Following Latitia's placement with her Aunt LaVrene and Uncle Willie, the protective services unit was able to close the case and terminate social services to the Phillips family.

T. 5. Data show that at least 35 percent of all BSW social workers are employed in child and family services.

T. 6. Most income assistance workers do not have social work training and thus are not social workers.

F. 7. The resources available to and used by social workers are always limited by the resources available within the immediate community.

T. 8. Social workers are the professionals who supervise foster homes.

T. 9. Adoption provides children and their adoptive parents the same legal rights and responsibilities with respect to one another as biological parenting.

F. 10. Most children become available for adoption as a result of the involuntary termination of the rights of their natural parents.

F. 11. Even when the identity of both biological parents is known, only the mother's written agreement is required for the voluntary termination of parental rights.

T. 12. Persons seeking to adopt a child privately through an attorney are required to have a home study.

T. 13. Group home care may meet a particular child's needs better than a foster home.

T. 14. Among the trends in institutional care for children has been a decrease in the use of orphanages.

T. 15. The idea that children have rights is quite new.

F. 16. Full-time employment at current minimum wage levels provides a family income that is just barely in excess of the poverty level.

F. 17. Research suggests that a residual approach to social welfare best meets the needs of children and families.

Fill-In

1. An attorney assigned by a court to represent the best interests of a legal minor is known as a (guardian ad litem).

2. Services to children and families can be divided into the two categories of (in-home) and (out-of-home) services.

3. The best professional education for entry into the field of child and family services is a (social work degree).

4. According to statistics collected by the National Center for Abuse and Neglect, the total number of abused and neglected children today is (more than one million).

5. Children who let themselves into their home after school hours and spend part of the day alone are known as ("latch key") children.

6. Out-of-home services are especially likely to be considered appropriate when a child's or family's needs are (long term).

7. The earliest form of substitute care for children was (in a relative's home).

8. The home of Latitia Phillips' aunt and uncle had to be (licensed) before she could be placed with them by the County Department of Social Services.

9. Residential treatment centers typically provide a program of behavior modification that encompasses the child's total environment and is sometimes known as (milieu therapy).

10. Formal public services to protect children were first mandated by law in the United States in the year (1974).

11. One of the first major social work texts to focus on the family as the primary unit of intervention was (Mary Richmond's **Social Diagnosis**).

12. The total number of children living in poverty in the United States in 1989 was approximately (13 million).

13. Research on the effectiveness of intervention in dealing with at-risk family situations seems to show than any family counseling approach is effective provided there is (a positive relationship between worker and clients).

Short Essay

1. Describe how the eligibility criteria for financial aid affected Latitia Phillips' family situation.

2. Explain why George Petit eventually determined that placement with relatives was the best possible feasible outcome for Latitia Phillips.

3. Describe the impact of the national trend to "declassify" professional social service jobs on the employment of social workers and the delivery of services.

4. List the basic steps required in a foster home study.

5. Explain why the belief that the 1989 welfare reform bill will liberate women from the welfare "trap" is a fallacy.

Essay

1. Explain how George Petit applied the principle of client self determination in the case of Latitia Phillips.

2. Define both in-home and out-of-home services to children and families and provide at least five examples of each type of service.

3. Compare and contrast the generalist work carried out by a protective services worker with family therapy.

4. Using examples and research findings presented in the text, draw up a proposal for an "ideal family policy."

CHAPTER 5. SUBSTANCE ABUSE: PREVENTION AND TREATMENT

Chapter Outline

Dan Graves (case study)
Understanding a Society that Uses/Abuses Chemicals
Patterns and Effects of Abuse
Roles for Social Workers
    Assessment
    Selecting the Means of Intervention
    Addressing the Needs of Special Populations
Building a Knowledge Base
The Social Worker's Values and Attitudes on Abuse: A Historical Perspective
Prevention and Treatment Settings
Alcoholics Anonymous and Other Self-Help Groups
Chemical Dependency: Societal Values, Social Policy, and Research
Summary

Learning Objectives

After reading Chapter 5, the student should be able to:

1. Cite evidence from the case study to show how abuse of alcohol had negative ramifications on the life of Dan Graves and others.

2. Explain why women, minorities, and homosexual persons may feel uncomfortable in AA meetings or other substance abuse programs.

3. Discuss alcohol abuse among women and explain why research data concerning the rate of alcoholism among women may, as yet, be unreliable.

4. List the most commonly used narcotics in the United States today; identify the methods of administration and the potential hazards of use for each.

5. Distinguish central nervous system stimulants from central nervous system depressants by their action on the human body and by their potential hazards and side effects.

6. Explain why not all persons with drinking disorders will necessarily have to refrain from drinking for the rest of their lives.

7. Explain why alcohol is a depressant, not a stimulant as it is often believed to be.

8. Define primary, secondary, and reactive alcoholism.

9. List 4 advantages of group intervention with substance abuse clients.

10. Give an example to illustrate how social workers practicing from a generalist perspective might target an organization for change rather than individual substance abusers or their families.

11. Explain the history and philosophy of Alcoholics Anonymous.

12. Discuss the public policy of the Bush and Reagan administrations concerning drugs.

13. Define longitudinal research study.

14. Define cross-addiction.

Additional Reading Materials

Dorris, M. The Broken Cord (New York: Harper and Row).

Haus, A., ed. Working with Homeless People: A Guide for Staff and Volunteers (New York: Columbia University Community Services, 1988).

Kinney, J., ed., and P. Kurzman, contributing ed. Bibliography and Resource Guide on Alcohol and Other Drugs for Social Work Educators (Rockville, MD: Office for Substance Abuse Prevention. Alcohol, Drug Abuse, and Mental health Administration. Public Health Service. U. S. Department of Health and Human Services, 1989).

Royce, J. E. Alcohol Problems and Alcoholism: A Comprehensive Survey 2nd ed. (New York: The Free Press, 1989).

"Special Issue on Homelessness," Social Work 34 (November 1989).

Van Warmer, K. "Training Social Work Students for Practice with Substance Abusers: An Ecological Approach," Journal of Social Work Education 23 (Spring/-Summer 1987): 47-56.

Watts, T. D. and Wright, R., Jr., eds. Alcoholism in Minority Populations (Springfield, IL: Charles C. Thomas, 1989).

Class Activities

1. Over a four day weekend, ask students to keep a diary noting all overheard or observed references to or use of alcohol and drugs including those that occur during social interactions with family or friends, are observed on television or in the movies, heard in songs on the radio, occur during shopping forays, etc. Ask for volunteers to share vignettes from their diaries with the class.

2. Have students form into two groups, groups A and B. Allow each group 25 minutes to discuss the relative advantages of individual and family work vs. group treatment with substance abusers. Then have Group A present the advantages of individual and family intervention and Group B the advantages of group treatment. As a variation of this exercise, form a third group, Group C, to discuss and present their views of the advantages of rehabilitation vs. punishment (deterrence) for substance abusers.

3. Provide students with copies of the Twelve Steps from AA and have individual students around the room read these aloud. Then ask students to simulate the "personal testimony" process by writing on the chalkboard, "My name is _____. I am a recovering procrastinator. It's been _____ (length of time) since I procrastinated. When I actively had this problem, I _____." Encourage class discussion of these student statements. Following the session, discuss the strengths and weaknesses of the self-help process.

Note: If the class is small, modify the above procedures by treating the class as a single group and asking each person, in turn, to share their "personal testimony" using the format provided above.

TEST ITEMS

Multiple-Choice

c) 1. Dan Graves in the case study on drug and substance abuse first started drinking:
   a. with his wife
   b. with co-workers
   c. with high school friends
   d. with other homeless people on the street

b) 2. Dan was first able to admit to being an alcoholic:
   a. when he was found on the street by police
   b. when he attended an Alcoholics Anonymous meeting at the hospital
   c. when he spoke with Madeleine Johnson, the Salvation Army social worker
   d. when he called his wife

b) 3. Madeleine Johnson, the Salvation Army social worker, was well prepared to help Dan with his alcohol abuse problem because of all but which one of the following:
   a. she had a BSW degree
   b. like Dan, she was also a black person
   c. she was a recovering alcoholic
   d. she had four years experience at the Emergency Lodge

c) 4. As Madeleine Johnson counseled Dan in the Salvation Army Lodge, she explored his feelings and views concerning all but which one of the following:
   a. the lack of resources available to poor people
   b. the death of his friend George
   c. neglect and abuse during Dan's early childhood
   d. the prejudice against black people Dan encountered in his AA group

d) 5. Madeleine Johnson used all but which one of the following skills in building a working relationship with Dan:
   a. confronting
   b. setting of limits
   c. self-disclosure
   d. role playing

33

a) 6. When Dan left the Salvation Army shelter, his immediate plans included AA attendance and which of the following:
    a. attending college and doing volunteer work
    b. mending his marriage and moving back in with his wife, Angie
    c. living on the streets, this time in a different area
    d. living in a halfway house and looking for work

a) 7. Sex-role stereotyping is widely believed to play a major role in contributing to which of the following behavior patterns:
    a. the historical tendency of men to consume more alcohol than women
    b. women's greater frequency of arrest for public drunkenness
    c. the fact that women are more likely than men to admit to alcoholism
    d. the ability of men "to handle" alcoholism better than women

d) 8. The most widely used central nervous system depressant is:
    a. phenobarbital
    b. cocaine
    c. peyote
    d. alcohol

c) 9. According to the chart in the text, which of the following is not a hallucinogen:
    a. LSD
    b. mescaline
    c. marijuana
    d. psilocybin

a) 10. Since 1985, physicians have had legal permission to use which of the following substances when treating cancer patients:
    a. marijuana
    b. heroin
    c. morphine
    d. valium

c) 11. Selection of a specific intervention plan in any area of social work practice is based on:
    a. referral information
    b. client self-determination
    c. assessment
    d. evaluation of the client's progress

a) 12. The client who "lives to drink" has:
    a. primary alcoholism
    b. secondary alcoholism
    c. reactive alcoholism
    d. subconscious alcoholism

a) 13. There is often a strong family history of alcoholism in:
    a. primary alcoholism
    b. female alcoholism
    c. reactive alcoholism
    d. teen-age alcoholism

c)   14. Mary Richmond suggested in her 1917 text, <u>Social Diagnosis</u>, that the word "inebriety" be used to replace the term:
a.   alcoholism
b.   intoxication
c.   drunkenness
d.   moral insufficiency

b)   15. The Alcohol, Drug Abuse, and Mental Health Administration (ADAMHA) is part of the:
a.   National Institute of Mental Health (NIMH)
b.   Public Health Service
c.   Bureau of Indian Affairs
d.   U.S. Surgeon General's Office

c)   16. Alcoholics Anonymous was founded in:
a.   1906
b.   1926
c.   1935
d.   1955

b)   17. Research by George and Carolyn Vaillant has demonstrated that the following are significant predictors of alcoholism:
a.   age of onset and type of drinking
b.   heredity and ethnicity
c.   ethnicity and age
d.   socialization experiences and stress tolerance levels

True-False

T   1. In the case study in chapter 5, Dan Graves first attended meetings of Alcoholics Anonymous while in the hospital.

F   2. Dan Graves was required to attend AA meetings weekly while living at the Salvation Army Lodge.

T   3. Dan's first job after leaving the Lodge was in a fast food restaurant.

T   4. After the repeal of Prohibition in 1933, alcohol use increased steadily until the 1970s.

F   5. Alcohol consumption in Third World countries has gradually declined over the past 20 years.

T   6. Reliable empirical data on the number of women who abuse alcohol and other substances is not yet readily available.

T   7. Simultaneous dependency on two or more drugs is known as <u>cross-addiction</u>.

T   8. Alcoholism counselors are themselves usually persons who are recovering from alcoholism or drug addiction.

T   9. Intervention essentially means problem-solving.

F   10.   Group treatment is the method of choice for all chemically dependent persons.

T   11.   Social workers whose practice is guided by a generalist perspective may select an organization rather than an individual or group as the target for change.

F   12.   Membership in Alcoholics Anonymous has been open to both women and men since the group's founding.

F   13.   Some social workers serve Alcoholics Anonymous in a professional capacity.

T   14.   Research shows that substance abuse prevention programs which are limited to providing information to school children have been ineffective in changing their behavior.

Fill-In

1. Extreme loss of body temperature is known as (hypothermia).

2. Distilled spirits are beverages that contain more than (14) percent alcohol.

3. A recovering alcoholic is one who (is no longer abusing alcohol) and is dealing with the awareness of her or his addiction on a (daily) basis.

4. The first organization founded in the United States to educate and lobby for legislation to reduce alcohol abuse was (The Women's Christian Temperance Union).

5. The Eighteenth Amendment, which prohibited the manufacture and sale of alcoholic beverages in the United States, was passed in (1919) and repealed in (1933).

6. The condition in which the unborn child is damaged by the mother's alcoholism is known as (fetal alcohol syndrome).

7. Examples of narcotics which are available by prescription are (morphine) and (codeine).

8. The illegal drug used in the greatest quantity today is (cocaine).

9. Some social workers have avoided working with substance abuse clients because of the frequency of (users' denials that they have a problem).

10. The central principles which guide the actions of AA members are known as (The Twelve Steps).

Short Essay

1. Identify and briefly describe the populations which are most vulnerable to substance abuse.

2. Describe, and provide at least two examples of, the ways in which media influence has contributed to awareness of substance abuse.

3. List the major policy recommendations which have resulted to date from national research on the effectiveness of federal, state, and local drug prevention programs.

Essay

1. Identify and discuss at least four areas you feel must be investigated when preparing a social work assessment of an alcoholic.

2. Select and describe three approaches that may be used in social work intervention with the alcoholic client and compare and contrast the way in which they may be used.

3. Identify and explain the differences between primary, secondary, and reactive alcoholism.

4. Discuss the advantages and disadvantages of group treatment of alcoholics.

5. Identify and describe the major emphases and approaches of current federal substance abuse prevention and treatment programs.

CHAPTER 6. SOCIAL WORK IN THE SCHOOLS

Chapter Outline

Lisa and Loretta Santiago (case study)
Impact of Cultural Diversity in the Schools
Social Work Roles in the Schools
Knowledge, Values, and Skills Related to Teamwork in the Schools
    Involvement in Special Education
    Values and Skills in Education
Educational Evaluations as Applied Research
Social Work Values in the School Setting: Policy Implications
History of Social Work in the Schools
    The Thirties Through the Fifties
    The Sixties and Seventies
    Trends
Summary

Learning Objectives

After reading Chapter 6, the student should be able to:

1. Identify current issues involving cultural diversity in the public schools.

2. Define culture and subculture.

3. Using the case study, define norms and describe how they may affect social work practice in the schools.

4. Using the case study, describe the generalist roles of school social workers.

5. Discuss the role of social workers in special education programs in the schools.

6. Discuss shifts of emphasis in school social work over the past several decades with respect to community intervention versus individual adjustment.

7. Identify the impact of values on the development of educational policy, e.g. bilingual programs, special education programs, and truancy procedures.

8. Discuss special education evaluations as examples of applied research.

9. Discuss the concept of accountability in school social work.

10. Describe how school social workers work as members of teams.

Additional Reading Materials

Allen-Meares, P. and K. J. Moroz. "Interfacing the Professions of Social Work and Education," Arete 14 (1989): 22-31.

Aguilar, I. "Initial Contact with Mexican-American Families," Social Work 17 (1972): 66-70.

Bogal-Albritten, R. B. "School Practice Course Work in the Social Work Curriculum," Social Work in Education 6 (1984): 221-230.

Brown, L. B., Otevier, J., and Klor de Alva, J. J., eds. A Resource Guide for Human Service Professionals: Sociocultural and Service Issues in Working with Hispanic American Clients (New York: Rockefeller College Press, 1985).

Davis, L. E. and Proctor, E. K. Race, Gender and Class: Guidelines for Practice with Individuals, Families and Groups (Englewood Cliffs, NJ: Prentice-Hall, 1989).

NASW Commission on Education. Expanding School Social Work: Through Federal Funding in Public Law (Silver Spring, MD: National Association of Social Workers, 1989).

Ruiz, R. "Cultural and Historic Perspectives in Counseling Hispanics," in D. W. Sue, ed. Counseling the Culturally Different (New York: John Wiley and Sons, 1981).

Class Activities

1. Ask each student to bring to class one or more recent newspaper articles that discuss issues involving children and schools. Ask for volunteers to share their articles with the class, then have the class discuss the ways in which social workers might address the issues presented in these articles.

2. Form the students into groups and ask each group to identify and discuss: a) the distinguishing social and cultural characteristics of the Santiago family; and b) the knowledge, values, and skills employed by Frank Haines, the school social worker, in his attempt to engage the various members of the family in problem-solving. Following the group discussions, ask each group to share their conclusions with the class.

3. To increase student sensitivity to the importance of subcultures, begin by pointing out that many different subcultures exist with the class. Then ask the students to form into groups based on common affiliations such as those who live on campus in residence halls, those who commute to campus, those who are employed, those who are parents, etc. Ask each group to identify and discuss the advantages and disadvantages of membership in their particular "subculture" with particular attention to any resulting stress that affects their daily life and activities and have each group report its findings to the class. If time permits, you may then wish to identify common themes which emerge from the group presentations and lead a class comparison of these with the experiences of other subcultures within our society.

4. Invite a school social worker to come to class and discuss some or all of the following aspects of his or her work: a) participation in evaluations for special education; b) the liaison role between child, school, and community; c) specific social work knowledge, values, and skills that he or she most frequently utilizes; and d) issues with which he or she is currently particularly concerned.

5. To prepare for a class discussion of bilingual education, have each student bring to class information obtained from one or more of the following sources: a) a faculty member involved with bilingual education; b) a local school social worker; c) a school administrator or school board member; or d) newspaper or magazine articles. Ask for volunteers to present the information they have obtained. Then lead a class discussion that focuses on major issues and possible solutions.

TEST ITEMS

Multiple-Choice

c) 1. Lisa and Loretta Santiago were referred to Frank Haines, the social worker in a bilingual junior high, because they had:
   a. been fighting on school property
   b. recently enrolled in the school after moving from Mexico
   c. been absent from school for 8 days
   d. been exposed to a communicable disease

d) 2. The bilingual education program described in the case study shared all but which one of the following characteristics:
   a. some classes taught entirely in Spanish
   b. a class in English as a Second Language (ESL)
   c. a teaching staff that included bilingual teachers
   d. an entirely Hispanic student body

c) 3. Frank Haines had an unusual interest and expertise in Hispanic culture because he had:
   a. grown up in a Hispanic neighborhood
   b. married a woman from a large Hispanic family
   c. travelled to Latin America and served as a youth worker with Hispanic youth
   d. lived in Ecuador for two years as a Peace Corps worker

a) 4. When Frank Haines visited the Santiagos, he was relieved that Mr. Santiago was at home with his wife because:
   a. in Hispanic cultures, it is often considered improper for an unrelated man to visit alone with a woman
   b. although Mr. Santiago could not speak English, his wife could and could thus translate for Frank
   c. a conference to assess the situation involving both parents was a school requirement
   d. he knew that Mr. Santiago was the dominant member of the family

b)   5. After Lisa and Loretta first ran away from home, they agreed to return
     when Mr. Santiago:
     a. went with them to a conference with the school principal
     b. stopped wearing his silver-studded black belt
     c. agreed that his daughters could have freedom in dating
     d. allowed his daughters to visit his ex-wife

d)   6. When Lisa and Loretta Santiago ran away from home a second time, Frank
     Haines made temporary arrangements for them to receive care from:
     a. relatives of their step-mother
     b. a residential treatment center for emotionally disturbed youth
     c. a group home
     d. the childrens protective services unit

a)   7. Frank Haines could not serve as primary therapist for family counseling
     with the Santiagos because:
     a. of a potential role conflict
     b. he did not hold an MSW degree
     c. he was not Hispanic
     d. he had not been able to establish a working relationship with Mr. San-
     tiago

c)   8. The advice given Lisa and Loretta by the family therapist in case their
     father became abusive was to:
     a. try and talk to him about their feelings
     b. stop running away from their problems
     c. give him "the silent treatment"
     d. call the school social worker immediately

d)   9. In order to do effective social work in a bilingual school setting,
     Frank Haines needed specific knowledge of all but which one of the follow-
     ing:
     a. sex role behavior and authority patterns in the Hispanic family
     b. dating customs that constrain Hispanic girls
     c. normal disciplinary practice in the Hispanic family
     d. the Hispanic family's disposition toward Anglos as providers of social
     work services in the schools

c)   10. The broad classification of social work services in schools known as
     "casework services to pupils" includes:
     a. working with families to enhance their parenting techniques
     b. establishing community groups to discuss special issues
     c. individual counseling of children referred by teachers
     d. educating and training school personnel to accept and participate in
     controversial programs

c)   11. The major ways in which the school setting affects the social worker's
     performance of his or her duties includes all but which one of the follow-
     ing:
     a. she or he is often the only social work professional in the setting
     b. the assigned responsibilities may include more than one school
     c. there is little opportunity for teamwork
     d. office space may have to be shared with other staff

a)   12. When one of the Santiago sisters, Lisa, was referred for special
          education evaluation, it was eventually determined that her problems were
          the result of:
          a. a short term reaction to stress in her family
          b. a chronic emotional disturbance of many year's duration
          c. mental retardation
          d. physical disabilities that limited her vision and hearing

a)   13. The history of social work in schools begins with efforts in:
          a. settlement houses
          b. the Charity Organization Society
          c. the Chicago Independent School District
          d. the Children's Aid Society

b)   14. Freudian psychology was accompanied by increased social work attention
          to:
          a. the causes of poverty
          b. the adjustment of the individual child
          c. stressful school conditions
          d. the need for large-scale social change

a)   15. Opportunities for social workers have expanded as a result of all but
          one of the following pieces of legislation:
          a. the Omnibus Budget Reconciliation Act
          b. the Economic Opportunity Act
          c. the Elementary and Secondary Education Act
          d. the Education for All Handicapped Children Act

True-False

T   1. Hispanics are the minority group which has been most successful at
          obtaining bilingual education.

F   2. Many school systems hired their first social worker only after the
          federal government passed a law requiring that counseling services be
          provided for at-risk students.

T   3. Today schools must offer special services for children found to have
          emotional disturbances.

F   4. A child whose behavior is abnormal in the school but not in the home is
          still classified by the school as emotionally disturbed.

T   5. Social workers are required to participate in all school evaluations for
          referral to special education programs.

T   6. Under current law, the written consent of the parents must be obtained
          before a child can be evaluated for special education.

T   7. Both Frank Haines and Ramon Garcia donated either time or services above
          that required by their job in order to assist the Santiago family.

T   8. Social work in the schools began with the efforts of voluntary social
          service organizations.

F   9. The earliest focus of school social work was on changing the behavior of problem children.

Fill-In

1. One of the key events that helped Frank Haines to understand the dynamics of the troubled relationship between Mr. Santiago and his daughters occurred when he (listened to a tape) provided by (Mr. Santiago).

2. A family service agency is an example of a (primary) setting for social work employment.

3. A school is an example of a (secondary--or host) setting for social work employment.

4. Public Law 94-142 requires that social workers (be a part of a team) that evaluates referrals for special education.

5. The Education for All Handicapped Children Act was passed in (1975).

6. Those workers who first began to provide social work services on behalf of school children were called (visiting teachers).

7. A set of standards for school social workers has been developed by (NASW).

8. The three major targets for services identified by current standards for school social work are (pupils and parents), (school personnel), and (the community).

Short Essay

1. Identify the members and responsibilities of the three different teams which worked with the Santiago family.

2. Identify and describe at least different types of needs of children who are referred for special education programs.

3. Describe the role of the social worker on a special education referral evaluation team.

4. Describe one major advantage and one major disadvantage for school social workers of the Education for All Handicapped Children Act.

Essay

1. Identify and discuss the benefits of bilingual education and the major obstacles to its implementation.

2. Identify and describe the social work values that Frank Haines applied when working with the Santiago family and illustrate each with an example.

3. Explain your understanding of the term applied research by describing how it might be conducted by a multidisciplinary special education team in a school setting.

CHAPTER 7. MENTAL HEALTH

Chapter Outline

John Winter (case study)
Knowledge, Values, and Skills Essential to Mental Health Work
    Areas of Responsibility
    Specific Knowledge Base
World Views, Values, and History of Native American People
Social Work Practice in Mental Health: Other Examples
    Community Practice
    Working for Change
Diversity and Range of Mental Health Practice Settings
Legislation, Litigation, and the Long History of Social Work Involvement
    Gradual Enlightenment
    The Influential Dorothea Dix
    The Twentieth Century
    Social Work Practice in Mental Health: Recent Shifts
Summary

Learning Objectives

After reading Chapter 7, the student should be able to:

1. Cite examples from the case study which demonstrate that Roberta Stokes, the social worker, valued and respected the culture and ethnicity of her Oneida Indian client, John Winter.

2. Explain the tasks and areas of responsibility of baccalaureate and master's degree social workers in the field of mental health.

3. Identify social work values that are important components of professional practice in mental health.

4. List 3 other professions that are members of the mental health team and differentiate their areas of responsibility from those of social work.

5. Explain what DSM-III-R is and what cautions must be observed by social workers when working with classification or labeling systems.

6. Explain how the Native American practices of talking circles and sings are potential resources for healing psychological wounds.

7. Identify 4 different mental health settings that employ social workers.

8. Describe the social reform work of Dorothea Lynde Dix.

9. Identify the mental health consequences of poverty that are particularly evident among racial and ethnic minorities and women.

10. Define psychotropic medication.

44

11. Define deinstitutionalization, explain how it came to be applied to mental hospitals in the united States, and identify and discuss its unintended results.

Additional Reading Materials

Bachrach, L. L., ed. Deinstitutionalization, New Directions for Mental Health Services (San Francisco: Jossey-Bass, 1983).

Dinges, N. G. Trimble, J. E., Manson, S. M., and Pasquale, F. L. "The Social Ecology of Counseling and Psychotherapy with American Indians and Alaskan Natives," in Marsella, A. J. and P. B. Pederson, eds. Cross-Cultural Counseling and Psychotherapy (New York: Pergamon Press, 1981), pp. 243-276.

Edwards, E. D. "American Indian/Alaskan Natives: Mental Health Issues and Social Work Training Needs," in Ethnic Minority Social Work Mental Health Clinical Training Programs: Assessing the Past-Planning for the Future (Washington, DC: National Institute of Mental Health, 1989).

LaFromboise, T. D., "American Indian Mental Health Policy," American Psychologist 43 (5): 388-397.

Class Activities

1. Form the class into groups to discuss the case of John Winter. Ask each group to identify the specific skills that reflected cultural sensitivity and were used by the social worker, Roberta Stokes, when working with John Winter. After allowing time for group discussion, ask a volunteer from each group to report on his or her group's findings.

2. To discuss labeling, have each student write down at least one word or term that they know (for a fact) has been used by others to describe them and drop their slip into a cardboard box, hat, or other container. Then draw these "labels" one at a time and read them to the class. As each is drawn, ask for class discussion of the effects (positive and negatives) such labels might have.

3. Divide the class into five groups and provide each with a copy of the DSM-III-R. Assign each of the five major axes (or dimensions) to a single group, and ask the group to prepare a summary of the major types of disorders associated with that axis. Have a member of each group report the group's findings to the class.

TEST ITEMS

Multiple-Choice

c) 1. John Winter, the psychiatric patient in the case study on mental health was a member of which of the following Native American groups:
    a. Mohawk
    b. Winnebago
    c. Oneida
    d. Cherokee

a)   2. John Winter's admitting diagnosis was:
       a. schizophrenia, chronic undifferentiated
       b. bipolar disorder
       c. post-traumatic stress syndrome
       d. schizophrenia, paranoid

d)   3. In building a working relationship with John Winter, Roberta Stokes used all but which one of the following skills:
       a. looking for strengths in the client
       b. interviewing
       c. pacing the discussion to the client's tempo
       d. hunting and fishing

c)   4. John Winter's socialization on the reservation had included all but which one of the following experiences:
       a. boarding school
       b. pow-wows
       c. initiation into a clan
       d. hunting and fishing

b)   5. In order to qualify for membership in the Academy of Certified Social Workers (ACSW), a social worker's training and experience must include all but which one of the following:
       a. an MSW degree
       b. at least one MSW-level field placement in a clinical setting
       c. at least two years direct supervision by an ACSW-level social worker
       d. a passing score on the national ACSW competency exam

a)   6. Today, the treatment of mental illness often consists of a combination of medication and:
       a. "talk therapy"
       b. confinement
       c. education
       d. environmental management

c)   7. The 1887 federal law that broke up many Native American reservations was the:
       a. Indian Reorganization Act
       b. Native Resettlement Ordinance
       c. General Allotment Act
       d. Indian Removal Act

b)   8. Historical evidence now suggests that the Great Law of Peace which governed the Six Nations of the Iroquois was the model for the:
       a. Declaration of Independence
       b. U.S. Constitution
       c. Charter of the United Nations
       d. Covenant of the League of Nations

d)   9. The group ritual used by the Navajo of the southwest to resolve problems is known as a:
       a. ghost dance
       b. sweat bath
       c. vision quest
       d. sing

b) 10. According to the social worker and researcher, John Red Horse, the members of a traditional Native American family are characterized by all but which one of the following:
a. the use of native language in the home and community
b. attendance and participation only in those social events and rituals that pertains to the family's specific tribal heritage
c. the practice of a native religion
d. acceptance of tribal beliefs about disease and health care

d) 11. Among the several types of Native American families, the type most likely to have a non-Indian concept of the cause of illness is known as:
a. neo-traditional
b. transitional
c. bicultural
d. acculturated

b) 12. A decline in the range of services offered by community mental health centers occurred in the 1980s because of:
a. the development of employee assistance programs in the workplace
b. the discontinuance of direct federal funding
c. a move into private practice by large numbers of mental health workers
d. their ineffectiveness in serving inner-city communities

d) 13. The first state hospital for the mentally ill in the United States was opened in:
a. Boston
b. Baltimore
c. Providence, Rhode Island
d. Williamsburg, Virginia

b) 14. "The first piece of social research ever conducted in America" was an 1843 report on the status of the mentally ill in Massachusetts prepared by:
a. Benjamin Rush
b. Dorothea Dix
c. Samuel Adams
d. Florence Nightingale

b) 15. The first social worker specifically hired to work with mentally ill patients was:
a. Ida Cannon
b. Mary Antoinette Cannon
c. Mary Richmond
d. Anna Freud

d) 16. The psychiatric social work training program initiated by Mary Jarrett in 1918 was located at what is now:
a. Bellevue Hospital in New York City
b. the Columbia University School of Social Work
c. the University of Chicago School of Social Service Administration
d. the Smith College School for Social Work

b)   17. The first major piece of federal mental health legislation was passed
in:
a.   1935
b.   1946
c.   1955
d.   1963

True-False

T   1. Roberta Stokes, the social worker in the John Winter case, held a BSW
degree.

T   2. One of the contributions frequently provided by the social worker who is
a member of a psychiatric assessment team is a better understanding of the
patient's cultural environment.

T   3. The social worker who is employed in a mental health setting is first of
all a social worker and secondly a mental health worker.

T   4. Social workers who provide crisis intervention and counseling services
at suicide prevention centers often have a BSW degree.

F   5. John Winter, the Oneida psychiatric patient, was reluctant to give the
social worker permission to share information about him with his family.

T   6. When John Winter was discharged from the psychiatric hospital, his
diagnosis remained the same as when he was initially admitted.

F   7. Social workers represent less than one-third of the mental health
professionals in the United States today.

F   8. Thus far, professional social workers have not been criticized for lack
of sensitive in their delivery of services to Native Americans.

T   9. Understanding the history and cultural systems of minority populations
helps social workers to respect the values and beliefs of the people with
whom they work.

F   10. Group work has not yet achieved acceptance as a method of treatment in
mental health settings that serve Native Americans.

T   11. The number of patients in state and county mental health hospitals
declined between 1960 and 1980.

F   12. Residential treatment centers for children are one type of mental
health setting that experienced growth in the 1980s.

T   13. Sigmund Freud taught that mental illness was the result of unresolved
conflicts.

T   14. By 1940, social workers were recognized members of mental health teams.

T   15. One of the activities of the National Institute of Mental Health (NIMH)
has been to provide funds for professional education in mental health work.

48

F   16. Despite budget cuts at the federal level, many states were able to expand their mental health programs during the 1980s.

Fill-In

1. The meetings where mental health professionals from several disciplines assemble to discuss new patients and develop treatment plans are called (staffings).

2. The first request made by John Winter to Roberta Stokes, the social worker in the psychiatric hospital, was to (be released from the hospital).

3. Drugs prescribed to influence a patient's mental functioning, mood, or behavior are known as (psychotropic) medications.

4. John Winter's mother communicated her caring for him during his hospitalization by sending (food--cornbread) to him.

5. Today, the term most commonly used for "psychiatric social worker" is (clinical social worker).

6. The psychiatric illness classification system that is most widely used by mental health professionals in the United States today is known as (DSM-III-R).

7. Under the Great Law of Peace, the code of justice that governed the Six Nations of the Iroquois, the judicial role was performed by (Women's Councils) acting as the equivalent of the U.S. Supreme Court.

8. One way that social workers in the mental health arena have used the media to effect community change has been through (appearances on television shows).

9. Access to psychiatric care among employed persons has increased because (many health insurance plans now cover treatment for psychiatric illness).

10. The 19th century social worker who became known for her lifelong devotion to establishing hospitals for the mentally ill was (Dorothea Dix).

11. The title of Clifford Beers' famous 1905 autobiographical account of his mental illness and treatment is (The Mind That Found Itself).

12. During its earliest years, the social work profession was split between two movements--the (settlement house) movement and the (Charity Organization Society).

13. The author of the first book on child psychotherapy published in 1933 was (Jessie Taft).

14. Psychiatric social services expanded during 1914-1918 and again during the 1940s because of (the number of soldiers who developed war-related mental disorders during these two periods).

15. NIMH stands for (National Institute of Mental Health).

16. The most important part of the 1961 Report of the Joint Commission on Mental Illness and Health was its emphasis on the need for (community-based facilities).

Short Essay

1. Briefly describe the content of the social assessment that social worker, Roberta Stokes, prepared on the psychiatric patient, John Winter.

2. Identify and describe the tasks involved in case management.

3. Identify the cultural influences that might have shaped John Winter's behavior and perceptions while in the hospital and describe how they might have contributed to the staff's belief that he was psychotic.

4. Describe how Roberta Stokes engaged John Winter in making decisions about his own post-hospitalization care.

5. Describe a "talking circle".

Essay

1. Identify and discuss the ways in which John Winter's social worker, Roberta Stokes, simultaneously intervened at the individual, family, hospital staff, and community levels.

2. Identify the four professions that are most frequently represented on a mental health team in a psychiatric hospital and describe the unique function(s) of each.

3. Discuss the advantages and disadvantages of using a diagnostic classification system such as DSM-III-R in mental health settings.

4. Identify and discuss the benefits and drawbacks associated with the mental health policy known as deinstitutionalization.

CHAPTER 8. DEVELOPMENTAL DISABILITIES AND SOCIAL WORK

Chapter Outline

The Several Roles of Stephanie Hermann, BSW (case study, part I)
    Stephanie's Educational Background
    Brockton Manor
Sandra McLean: The Effects of Institutionalization (case study, part II)
    Ongoing Challenges
Types of Developmental Disabilities
    Mental Retardation
    Cerebral Palsy
    Autism
    Orthopedic Problems
    Hearing Problems
    Epilepsy
    Learning Disabilities
    Co-Occurrence of Disabilities
Services for the Disabled: A Brief History
    Training Schools
    Protective Asylums
    Eugenics Movement
    Research Stimulates Change
    Normalization and the Deinstitutionalization Movement
    Deinstitutionalization Accelerates
    Human Diversity and Vulnerable Populations: Unfinished Business
Social Work Roles with Disabled People
NASW Standards for Service
Settings for Work with the Developmentally Disabled
Professional and Personal Values
Summary

Learning Objectives

After reading Chapter 8, the student should be able to:

1. Identify the differences between categorical and functional definitions of disability and explain their importance.

2. Understand what distinguishes a developmental disability from other types of disability.

3. Define and describe eight categories of developmental disability.

4. Describe three social factors that tended to demean people with disabilities in the late 1800s and early 1900s.

5. Describe how research helped demonstrate the competence of many disabled people.

6. Define normalization.

7. Discuss the concept of deinstitutionalization.

8. Identify how human diversity factors complicate the normalization and deinstitutionalization processes.

9. Identify and describe generalist roles for social work practitioners with the disabled.

10. Identify five NASW standards for service with the developmentally disabled.

11. Discuss why value issues in the field of developmental disabilities are especially complex.

Additional Reading Materials

Berdine, W. H. and Blackhurst, A. E., eds. An Introduction to Special Education 2nd ed. (Boston, MA: Little, Brown, 1985).

DeWeaver, K. L. "Producing Social Workers Trained for Practice with the Developmentally Disabled," Arete 7 (1982): 59-62.

Edgerton, R., Bollinger, M., and Herr, B. "The Cloak of Competence: After Two Decades," American Journal of Mental Deficiency 88 (1984): 345-351.

Horejsi, C. R. "Developmental Disabilities: Opportunities for Social Workers," Social Work 24 (1979): 79.

Kanale, K. and Forness, S. The Science of Learning Disabilities (San Diego, CA: College-Hill Press, 1985).

McDonald-Wikler, L. and Edwards, M. "Research in Mental Retardation: Some Relevant Issues for Researchers in Chronic Mental Illness," in Bowker, J. and A. Rubin, eds. Studies on Chronic Mental Illness: New Horizons for Social Work Researchers (Washington, DC: Council on Social Work Education, 1986).

Wikler, L. and Keenan, M. P., eds. Developmental Disabilities, No Longer a Private Tragedy (Silver Springs, MD: National Association of Social Workers and American Association on Mental Deficiency, 1983).

Class Activities

1. Ask for two teams of volunteers to research deinstitutionalization and participate in a debate on its merits in class, presenting the strongest arguments they can muster on behalf of their side of the case. Allow each side approximately 15 minutes for their presentation and then open the discussion to the entire class.

2. Form the class into three groups and ask each to write a feature length article on learning disabilities for the school paper. Have each group present its paper to the class for discussion and evaluation. Submit the best example to the paper.

Multiple-Choice

b)   1. The term, "developmental disability", is usually defined as including <u>all but which one</u> of the following:
a. mental retardation
b. mental illness
c. cerebral palsy
d. epilepsy

d)   2. In her position as an assistant administrator with the state Division of Community Services, Stephanie Hermann placed primary emphasis on the portion of her role concerned with:
a. enforcement of regulations
b. client advocacy
c. community education
d. agency consultation

a)   3. The change in federal regulations with which Stephanie Hermann's agency had to deal affected client eligibility for:
a. Medicaid
b. Social Security
c. Medicare
d. AFDC

b)   4. The primary objective of the changes in federal funding regulations described in the case involving Stephanie Hermann was to encourage:
a. the development of certified programs for developmentally disabled people by nursing homes
b. the development of community-based living arrangements for the developmentally disabled by states and counties
c. public hospitals to establish diagnostic facilities to serve the poor
d. the employment by states and counties of more social workers with expertise in the area of developmental disabilities

d)   5. Stephanie Hermann and her Subcommittee on Relocation carried out <u>all but which one</u> of the following tasks:
a. established teams to assess all developmentally disabled residents at Brockton Manor
b. conducted a study to determine the probable costs of community placement
c. organized and conducted a "stakeholders" meeting
d. conducted "fact-finding" tours to existing adult family care homes

b)   6. Sandra McLean's mental retardation was the result of:
a. a genetic disorder
b. an injury at birth
c. a closed head injury suffered during childhood
d. a drug taken by her mother during pregnancy

a)   7. Sandra McLean's ability to function deteriorated markedly while she was:
a. a resident of a state institution for the mentally retarded
b. living at home following the birth of her sister
c. enrolled in a community activity center during her teens
d. living in a nursing home

d) 8. The plan developed for Sandra McLean following an assessment and evaluation by a multi-disciplinary team called for her:
a. to be returned to her home where she could live with her mother
b. reclassification and transfer to a different part of the nursing home
c. placement in a supervised group home where she would live with three other mentally retarded women
d. placement in an adult family care home

c) 9. In order to qualify as a "developmental disability" under federal guidelines, the disabling condition must occur before the age of:
a. 12
b. 16
c. 22
d. 30

b) 10. The reformer who established the first American training schools for children with handicaps was:
a. Johann Guggenbubl
b. Samuel Greadley Howe
c. Francis Galton
d. Charles Loring Brace

b) 11. Sterilization of the retarded was advocated by:
a. the Social Darwinists
b. the Eugenicists
c. Benet and Simon
d. Margaret Sanger

a) 12. "Normalization" is a concept that was first developed:
a. in the Scandinavian countries in the 1950s.
b. in the Soviet Union shortly after the close of World War I
c. in France in the 1830s
d. in the United States at the turn of the century

c) 13. When the first wave of deinstitutionalization took place in the late 1960s and early 1970s, most developmentally disabled people removed from large state institutions were:
a. transferred to family care homes
b. transferred to small group homes
c. placed in nursing homes
d. simply put out on the street

c) 14. Services designed to help developmentally disabled individuals achieve their highest possible level of functioning are described as:
a. community-based
b. therapeutic milieu
c. habilitation
d. holistic

a) 15. Social workers in the field of developmental disabilities need to place more emphasis on their role in:
a. policy development and administration
b. discharge planning
c. counseling
d. making referrals

True-False

T   1. Stephanie Hermann, the social worker in the case on developmental disabilities, held two degrees, one in nursing and one in social work.

F   2. In Stephanie Hermann's state, per diem Medicaid payments for developmentally disabled persons in nursing homes were higher than per diem payments for mentally retarded persons in institutions.

T   3. Current estimates suggest there is a greater incidence of developmental disability among adults than among children.

F   4. Persons who become developmentally disabled as a result of accidents in mid-life are eligible for the same federal assistance payments as those whose condition is diagnosed in childhood.

T   5. A person with a mild disability that qualifies for "categorical" state aid will not automatically be eligible for federal assistance.

F   6. Cerebral palsy is always accompanied by at least a moderate level of mental retardation.

T   7. Current data on the co-occurrence of disabilities suggests that a majority of developmentally disabled persons suffer from only one disabling condition.

T   8. The Elizabethan Poor Law of 1601 provided limited food and shelter for people with handicaps.

T   9. Efforts to educate Victor, "the wild boy" of the early 1800s, were only partially successful.

F   10. The first facility for persons suffering from cretinism was established in the United States in 1907.

F   11. Throughout the 1800s, most U.S. training schools for developmentally disabled children were small facilities with a maximum capacity of 20.

T   12. By the 1930s, there were still only a limited number of community-based family care homes for the disabled in this country.

F   13. The economic climate of the 1970s hindered the deinstitutionalization movement.

T   14. Social workers who work with the developmentally disabled must of necessity be generalists.

T   15. Current trends in Medicaid and other related regulations suggest that federal funding to maintain people with developmental disabilities in inappropriate institutional settings is likely to be discontinued in the near future.

Fill-In

1. The initials ICF/MR stand for (intermediate care facility/mentally retarded).

2. Two ongoing problems faced by counties with respect to community care are inadequate (funding) and restrictive (zoning ordinances).

3. It is estimated that one child in (ten) in this country has a developmental disability.

4. Persons with IQ scores of (50-70) are usually classified as mildly retarded.

5. The autistic child who repeats what is said without comprehending its meaning has a type of speech known as ("echolalic").

6. Children who are unable to walk as a result of being born with an incomplete spinal column suffer from a condition known as (spina bifida).

7. The two types of seizures associated with epilepsy are (grand mal) and (petit mal).

8. The types of disabilities most often discovered after children begin attending school are (learning disabilities).

9. The first country to make a concerted effort to provide education for persons with disabilities was (France).

10. W.E. Fernald's 1919 study of over 1500 disabled residents who had been released from institutions showed that most exhibited (socially acceptable) behavior.

11. World War II improved public attitudes toward the disabled because of (the large number of veterans who returned home with handicaps).

12. The national voluntary agency which specializes in providing services and assistance to persons with mental retardation and their families is the (Association for Retarded Citizens).

13. The most recent President to publicly acknowledge that he had a relative with mental retardation was (John F. Kennedy).

14. Foster home-type arrangements that are designed to provide temporary, short-term relief for full-time care givers are known as (respite care) homes.

15. Professional guidelines for dealing with ethical dilemmas in social work practice are provided by the (NASW Code of Ethics).

Short Essay

1. Briefly explain what is meant by the statement, "For a given person to qualify for federal funds, his or her disability must be severe in function."

2. Explain the reasons why a large proportion of those children who are mildly retarded are found among the poor.

3. Briefly explain why IQ tests may not always accurately measure ability.

4. Explain why parents or legal guardians sometimes have mixed emotions when they learn community placement is being considered for their developmentally disabled child or ward.

Essay

1. Identify and describe each of the four roles played by Stephanie Hermann in responding to the emergency order from her state's Department of Health and Human Services concerning changes in Medicaid funding for people with developmental disabilities.

2. Identify and describe the major obstacles that currently hamper efforts to provide adequate services to the developmentally disabled in our society and explain how each might be overcome.

3. Explain why social work practice with the developmentally disabled requires a generalist orientation.

4. Using the Sandra McLean case from the chapter on developmental disabilities, identify and explain the types of ethical dilemmas that most frequently arise in the course of social work practice.

5. Define "normalization" as it applies to work with the developmentally disabled and describe its policy implications.

CHAPTER 9. CRIMINAL JUSTICE SETTINGS

Chapter Outline

Jeff Wagner (case study)
Components of the Criminal Justice System
    Law Enforcement
    The Courts
    The Correctional System
Social Work Intervention with Groups and Organizations
Value Dilemmas for Social Workers in Corrections
Public Policy and Criminal Justice
    The Prison Population
    Juvenile Justice
    The Mentally Ill Inmate
    The Death Penalty
    Minorities as Victims of Crime
Research
History of Social Work in Criminal Justice
Summary

Learning Objectives

After reading Chapter 9, the student should be able to:

1. Use examples from the case study to describe how a baccalaureate social worker might function with a young adult offender.

2. Identify the three components of the United States criminal justice system.

3. Explain the major responsibilities of police social workers.

4. Define presentence investigation.

5. Differentiate probation from parole.

6. Identify at least two potential value conflicts for social workers in correctional settings and explain how the NASW Code of Ethics guides the practice of social workers.

7. Describe social work practice within prisons.

8. Explain the social control function of probation and parole agents.

9. Discuss the use of imprisonment and the death penalty as effective deterrents to crime.

10. Referring to data from the Bureau of Justice in the text, demonstrate how minorities are victimized by crime.

11. Use an example from the text to show how research can help to answer questions related to crime and criminal offenders.

12. Identify at least three persons who were significant in the development of social work in criminal justice.

Additional Reading Materials

Crow, R. and McCarthy, G., eds. Teenage Women in the Juvenile Justice System (Tucson, AZ: New Directions for Young Women, 1979).

Inglehart, A. and Stein, M. "The Female Offender: A Forgotten Client," Social Casework 66 (March 1985): 152-159.

Johnson, H. W. "Crime, Delinquency, and Correction: Rural Perspectives," in A. Summers et al, eds., Social Work in Rural Areas, Proceedings of the 10th National Institute (Columbia, MO, 1987)

Klein, M., ed. The Juvenile Justice System (Newbury Park, CA: Sage Publications, 1987).

Murphy, J. W. and Dison, J. E. Are Prisons Any Better? Twenty Years of Correctional Reform (Newbury Park, CA: Sage Publications, 1990).

Shireman, C. H. and Reamer, F. G. Rehabilitating Juvenile Justice (New York: Columbia University Press, 1987).

Class Activities

1. Social workers employed in criminal justice settings are a source of particularly valuable first-hand information for students. Inviting any of one of the following to speak to your class will, therefore, be particularly rewarding: a police social worker, probation agent, parole officer, victim assistance program worker, prison social worker, or worker or director from a community-based facility. Suggest to your speaker that he or she focus on: a) the social work skills that are most important to his or her work; b) how he or she handles the use of authority; and c) the community resource networks he or she finds most valuable or uses most often. You may also find it useful to combine this type of presentation with a field trip, in which case the speaker may wish to address the class on site rather than in the classroom.

2. Form the class into four groups. Ask each group to "brainstorm" a list of ideas for making correctional facilities more humane and effective at rehabilitation. At the conclusion of the brainstorming session, ask one member of each group to report the group's ideas to the class.

3. A role play exercise is a useful way of clarifying the principles which guide the use of authority in social work practice, especially in mandated settings. One way to do this in connection with criminal justice is to ask for one or more sets of volunteers to play the roles of a social worker and a mandated client. Provide each volunteer with a copy of Table 4, "Principles to Guide Use of Authority in Social Work Practice", from page 285 of the text and a one page sheet that provides background information about their "character" or role, his or her immediate objectives, and a brief

synopsis of the circumstances that bring these two individuals together. Each set of volunteers should then conduct an interview before the class, either with or without an introduction by the instructor or a student volunteer. The task of each volunteer should be to act and respond as he or she believes his or her character would under the circumstances involved, which should emphasize the worker's attempt(s) to make appropriate use of his or her authority. If the facilities are available to do so, you may wish to videotape these role plays for subsequent discussion.

4. Ask each student to interview friends and associates concerning their views on the death penalty--whether they support or oppose it and why--and then to share his or her findings with the class. Ask the class to discuss the reasons behind the attitudes discovered and to compare these attitudes to social work values.

TEST ITEMS

Multiple-Choice

d) 1. Jeff Wagner, the young male offender in the case on criminal justice, was released from prison after serving eighteen months of a four year sentence for:
a. auto theft
b. burglary
c. drug possession
d. armed robbery

b) 2. When Jeff Wagner was released from prison, he had served only a portion of his sentence and:
a. was to serve the remainder while on probation
b. was to serve the remainder while on parole
c. was granted a reprieve from the remaining portion
d. had been given a suspension of his sentence

a) 3. In his initial meeting with Jeff Wagner, the probation officer, Alan Martin, reviewed with Jeff a document known as:
a. a parole contract
b. a court brief
c. a probation license
d. a suspended sentence

c) 4. The three major components of the American criminal justice system are sometimes known as the "three C's" which stands for:
a. cases, cops, and criminals
b. criminals, courts, and cells
c. courts, cops, and corrections
d. the three types of cases--civil, criminal, and constitutional

c) 5. The four major sources of law in the United States include all but which one of the following:
a. case law
b. constitutional law
c. civil law
d. administrative law

b) 6. The term probation refers to:
a. a specified period during which a prisoner is liable to an extension of his or her sentence if found guilty of further infractions
b. the suspension of imprisonment following conviction on the condition that the individual fulfills certain requirements
c. the release of a prisoner before completion of his or her full sentence
d. in misdemeanor cases, the period following conviction during which a defendant is allowed to remain at large pending the outcome of an appeal

c) 7. The term parole refers to:
a. a specified period during which a prisoner is liable to an extension of his or her sentence if found guilty of further infractions
b. the suspension of imprisonment following conviction on the condition that the individual fulfills certain requirements
c. the release of a prisoner before completion of his or her full sentence
d. in misdemeanor cases, the period following conviction during which a defendant is allowed to remain at large pending the outcome of an appeal

d) 8. It has been estimated that approximately what percent of all police work is noncriminal in nature:
a. 25%
b. 50%
c. 61%
d. 80%

a) 9. One of the most common duties performed by social workers employed in the court system is:
a. preparing presentence investigations
b. counseling jurors in felony cases
c. providing assistance to victims of violent crime
d. advising the court about prison conditions

d) 10. Which of the following is not one of the more commonly used alternative to imprisonment:
a. community service
b. restitution
c. the use of an electronic wrist or ankle bracelet
d. plea bargaining

c) 11. The unique contribution of social workers in correctional settings stems from:
a. their generalist perspective on the social problems associated with prison life
b. their daily contact and communication with prisoners, all levels of the prison staff, and many outsiders
c. their application of the NASW Code of Ethics
d. their function as a link between the prison staff and the public

b) 12. The key function of the social worker who functions as a probation agent or parole officer is to:
a. monitor the client's behavior as closely as possible
b. help the client meet the terms of the parole or probation agreement
c. report on client infractions of parole and probation agreements to correctional authorities
d. help the client qualify for a reduced sentence

a)   13. Group work has been found to be particularly effective in all but which one of the following settings:
a. the presentence interview
b. prison facilities
c. offenders outside of prison settings
d. community-based group homes for adolescent offenders

d)   14. Clients who are required by law to see a social worker or other professional person are called:
a. criminals
b. social offenders
c. probationary clients
d. mandatory clients

c)   15. The imprisonment rate in the United States is currently:
a. roughly the same as that in other western nations
b. slowly declining
c. at least double that of any western European country
d. less than 50 per 100,000 citizens

b)   16. The sentence for first degree murder in Sweden is approximately twenty-four months; in the United States it is commonly:
a. mandatory life imprisonment
b. twenty years to life
c. ten to twenty years
d. capital punishment

a)   17. Both blacks and Hispanics tend to be overrepresented as victims of crime and in:
a. reports of arrests, convictions, and imprisonment
b. reports of injuries resulting from unprovoked racial assaults
c. reports of crime-related losses of personal property
d. criminal justice statistics generally

d)   18. Data confirms the existence of racial bias in arrests and suggests that this bias reflects the attitudes of both the arresting officer and:
a. the suspected offender
b. the local court system
c. local media
d. the citizen making the complaint

c)   19. Juvenile courts first began to be established across the United States during the:
a. Revolutionary War
b. late 1830s
c. early 1900s
d. 1960s

b)   20. Two prominent figures who provided much of the leadership, teaching, and research in the early days of correctional social work in this country were:
a. Ida Cannon and Mary Richmond
b. Jane Addams and Edith Abbott
c. Elliot Studt and Harvey Treger
d. John Augustus and Alexander Maconochie

<u>True-False</u>

T   1. Jeffrey Wagner was only 18 years old when he was sentenced to a four year term for armed robbery.

T   2. As part of his parole agreement, Jeff Wagner was required to report <u>once a month</u> to his parole officer, Alan Martin.

T   3. The major goals of the criminal justice system are to punish, to deter crime, to rehabilitate, and to remove criminals from society.

F   4. A misdemeanor is a relatively minor offense, a "misdeed", which results in no legal consequences for the offender.

T   5. A felony is a serious crime such as murder, rape, or armed burglary.

F   6. Police officers have very little decision making responsibility.

F   7. Parole and probation are essentially identical concepts.

T   8. Police social work is a relatively underdeveloped area of social work practice that has demonstrated growth in recent years.

F   9. All but a small fraction of suspects initially detained for questioning are ultimately convicted and sentenced.

T   10. Social workers are generally not directly involved in the decision-making concerning prosecution.

T   11. Social workers have been directly responsible for establishing some restitution programs.

T   12. Each of the fifty states has its own correctional system with varying structures, sanctions, and administrative laws.

F   13. The two major components of most correctional systems are prisons and courts.

F   14. All prison staffs are now required by federal law to include a minimum number of social workers.

T   15. Most, although not all, probation and parole agents are BSW or MSW social workers.

T   16. Probation and parole agents often have very large caseloads.

T   17. Social workers use assertiveness training to help groups of prisoners communicate their anger to guards as well as to other inmates in ways that will not cause them to be attacked.

T   18. Group homes for offenders tend to have a very high rate of staff turnover because of staff "burnout".

T 19. Forcing a client to see a social worker on a regular basis can result in "conning" where the client learns to tell the worker what he or she wants to hear and nothing more.

F 20. The trend toward increasing incarceration in the United States has made the streets of the nation's cities safer as indicated by declining crime rates.

Fill-In

1. Law which is made up of the rules and regulations developed by federal and state executive agencies in order to carry out statutory laws is known as (administrative law).

2. The term case law refers to the published decisions of (courts).

3. The police are responsible for keeping the peace and for responding to (criminal complaints).

4. A court in which witnesses and defendants are subject to cross-examination by a prosecutor and a defense attorney is a(n) (adversarial) court.

5. A sentence of capital punishment is one involving (the death penalty).

6. Punishment inflicted on the body is known as (corporal punishment).

7. An offense that is limited to only certain groups or categories of persons such as children is known as a (status offense).

8. A correctional facility that is generally used for short sentences or for detaining persons while they await a court hearing is known as a (jail).

9. Restitution programs are programs that require a convicted offender to (restore) to a person something that was stolen, removed, damaged, or destroyed.

10. The act of returning a paroled person to prison, thereby cancelling parole, is known as (revocation).

Short Essay

1. Identify and define the four major sources of law that govern the criminal justice system in the United States.

2. Briefly define and explain the differences between parole and probation.

3. List at least three types of decisions that may be made once a person has been arrested.

4. List the steps of the problem-solving process as used by Alan Martin in his work with Jeffrey Wagner.

5. Briefly list the major arguments for and against the use of the death penalty.

Essay

1. What are the major sources of frustration for social workers employed in criminal justice settings? How can each of these best be dealt with?

2. Should social workers become more heavily involved with criminal justice policy? Why or why not?

3. How realistic do you think the outcome of the Jeffrey Wagner case in chapter nine is? Why?

4. Do we know whether minorities actually commit more crime? Why or why not? If so, what does this mean to social workers?

CHAPTER 10. SOCIAL WORK WITH THE ELDERLY

Chapter Outline

Rose Balistrieri (case study)
Who Are the Elderly?
    Geographical Distribution
    Marital Status
    Employment and Economic Status
    Health and Mental Health
    Ethnicity
    Housing
Research on Family Strengths
    Intergenerational Stress and Cultural Conflict Within Families
Societal Services to the Elderly--Past to Present
    Family Care
    Pension Plans
    Other Federal Entitlement Programs
    Housing Assistance
    Health Insurance
    Food Stamps
More Federal Legislation Relating to the Elderly
    The Older Americans Act
    The Social Services Block Grant
Values and Public Policy
"Continuum of Care" Concept: Prolonging Independence
    Importance of Generalist Social Work
    Components of Care
Work with the Elderly: A Growing Future
Summary

Additional Reading Materials

Cox, E. O., Parsons, R. J., and Kimboko, P. J.   "Social Services and Intergenerational Caregivers: Issues for Social Work," Social Work 33 (1988): 430-434.

Dobrof, R., ed.   Social Work and Alzheimer's Disease (Binghamton, NY: Haworth Press, 1986).

Hancock, B. L.   Social Work with Older People 2nd ed. (Englewood Cliffs, NJ: Prentice-Hall, 1990).

Hooyman, N. R. and Lustbader, W.   Taking Care of Your Aging Family Members (New York: The Free Press, 1988).

Lowy, L.   Social Work with the Aging 2nd ed. (White Plains, NY: Longman, 1985).

Monk, A., ed.   "Health Care Needs of the Aged," Journal of Gerontological Social Work, Special Issue 15 (1990)

Moxley, D. P.   The Practice of Case Management (Newbury Park, CA: Sage Publications, Inc., 1989).

Silverstone, B., et al. Social Work Practice with the Frail Elderly and Their Families (Springfield, IL: Charles C. Thomas, 1983).

"The Daughter Track," Newsweek (July 16, 1990): 48-54

Learning Objectives

After reading Chapter 10, the student should be able to:

1. Identify approximately how many Americans will be 65 by the year 2000, and what percent they will be of the total population.

2. Discuss at least three reasons why advanced age is usually more of a problem for women than for men.

3. Identify what percent of the elderly receive over half their income from Social Security.

4. Identify the percent of all elderly who fall in the "near-poor" category, and which groups of elderly are most vulnerable to poverty.

5. Discuss the concept of "house-poor".

6. Discuss the concept of "intimacy at a distance" that research indicates many elderly prefer with respect to their children.

7. Describe the "crunch" in which middle aged children often find themselves with respect to their own parents and children.

8. Define entitlement program.

9. Identify four federal entitlement programs designed to assist the elderly.

10. Identify four value-related issues that will shape the direction of future social policy for the elderly.

11. Discuss the concepts of continuum of care and least restrictive environment.

12. Using this chapter's case study, describe generalist social work roles with the elderly.

Class Activities

1. Form the class into three groups to review Jake Jacobs' handling of the Rose Balistrieri case in this chapter. Have the first group identify the social work values that influenced Jake, the second group identify specific examples of his use of social work knowledge, and the third group identify the specific intervention skills he used. Have each group report its findings to the class.

2. Using the list of services on pages 323-324 of the text, assign each of these to a single student (or group of students) and ask the students to research the availability of the service involved in the local community, where possible identifying the specific agencies from whom the services are available. Ask each student to report his or her findings to the class.

3. If your class contains older students who have had direct experience with the intergenerational care of elderly relatives, ask these students to participate in a panel discussion in which they share some of their experiences with the class. In order to identify common themes, positive feelings, sources of frustration, policy related issues, and areas where additional local resources are needed, either moderate the discussion or ask for a volunteer to do so.

TEST ITEMS

Multiple-Choice

c) 1. In the case vignette on social work with the elderly, social worker Jake Jacobs was employed by an agency which was:
   a. public, nonprofit
   b. private, for profit
   c. private, nonprofit
   d. public, for profit

a) 2. Most of the clients served by Jake's agency were:
   a. white females
   b. Hispanic and black females
   c. white males
   d. black males

d) 3. The most important service offered by the agency was:
   a. recreation through a senior center
   b. support groups
   c. food and shelter
   d. case management

d) 4. The client, Ms. Balistrieri, received limited assistance from her children because of all but which one of the following:
   a. her son was physically handicapped
   b. a daughter lived over a thousand miles away
   c. a daughter was a mental patient
   d. a son still lived in Italy

b) 5. In assessing Ms. Balistrieri's needs, Jake Jacobs explored her eligibility for all but which one of the following services:
   a. subsidized housing
   b. medical care
   c. a volunteer to visit and provide transportation
   d. "meals on wheels"

68

a) 6. Jake Jacobs felt Ms. Balistrieri should accept the services for which she qualified because he believed:
a. they were hers by right
b. elderly people deserve charity
c. she had the funds to pay for them
d. his agency needed additional clients

a) 7. Ms. Balistrieri did not qualify for Supplemental Security Income:
a. because her monthly income exceeded the limit allowed
b. because she was living independently
c. because her physical condition was not serious enough
d. because she refused to apply

c) 8. Following a visit to the landlord, Ms. Balistrieri concluded that
a. she would not need further services
b. her rights as a tenant would be upheld
c. she might need to move
d. she would stay in the building, tolerating the noise

b) 9. According to Maldonado's classification of the elderly, the "old" are:
a. persons between the ages of 55-64
b. persons between the ages of 65-74
c. persons between the ages of 75-84
d. persons who are 85 or older

d) 10. The elderly are still under-represented in which one of the following:
a. central cities
b. places in warm climates
c. metropolitan locations
d. suburban areas

d) 11. The percent of the elderly who receive Social Security income today is:
a. 50%
b. 73%
c. 84%
d. over 90%

a) 12. The first country to initiate a compulsory pension program was:
a. Germany
b. France
c. Australia
d. England

b) 13. Jake Jacobs and his agency were successful in a community organizing effort to obtain for the frail elderly:
a. additional low income housing
b. a subsidized cab service
c. a "meals on wheels" program
d. representation on the city council

c) 14. It is increasingly recognized that elderly people can benefit from:
a. living with their children
b. religious experiences
c. mental health counseling
d. making a living will

c)   15.   In-home services to the elderly include all but which one of the
following:
a.   yard work and house cleaning
b.   volunteer visits
c.   congregate meals
d.   telephone monitoring

a)   16.   The best rationale for making home care available to the elderly is
that it is:
a.   more humanitarian
b.   more cost effective
c.   easier to develop and coordinate
d.   covered by both Medicare and Medicaid

True-False

T   1.   A smaller proportion of elderly men are employed today than were
employed in 1950.

F   2.   Among whites, elderly men are twice as likely as women to be poor.

T   3.   In a 1984 Senate Special Committee on Aging report, a majority of elderly
persons described their health as good or excellent.

F   4.   The numbers of white elderly are growing at a faster pace than black and
Hispanic elderly.

T   5.   Research demonstrates that most children do a great deal for their aging
parents.

T   6.   Most elderly never receive private pensions.

T   7.   Applications for SSI benefits are made through federal Social Security
offices.

F   8.   Housing assistance programs for the elderly do not require specific
levels of income for eligibility.

F   9.   Medicaid benefits for the poor are uniformly controlled by national
eligibility standards.

T   10.   Only about ten percent of current users of food stamps are elderly.

T   11.   Personal care homes differ from nursing homes in the amount of nursing
care available.

T   12.   Increasing numbers of elderly persons face moving to a nursing home.

T   13.   Medicaid provides more flexibility in funding nursing home care than
Medicare.

1. The bone thinning disease commonly found in frail elderly women is called (osteoporosis).

2. The agency which employed Jake Jacobs was sponsored and funded by (inner city churches).

3. The greatest amount of Ms. Balistrieri's monthly income was spent on (housing).

4. Ms. Balistrieri's initial response to Jake's suggestion that she consider applying for subsidized housing was to (protest).

5. The number of Americans over age 65 is growing and by the year 2000 will number approximately (35 million).

6. Today, mandatory retirement takes place at age (70).

7. Increasing attention has been given to the condition which causes mental confusion in adults known as (Alzheimer's disease).

8. Approximately (70) percent of the elderly own their own homes.

9. The majority of the caretakers who provide extensive and intensive assistance to older relatives are (women).

10. Supplemental Security Income is funded by (general tax revenues).

11. The most important legislation of the 1960s for persons over 60 was the (Older Americans) Act.

12. A voluntary organization that regularly lobbies congress to increase funding for the elderly is the (American Association of Retired Persons).

13. In 1983, the bulk of federal spending for the elderly went for (Social Security payments), (Medicare), and (Medicaid).

Short Essay

1. Describe what is meant by "an entitlement program" and give two examples.

2. Define "policy making" and describe how it begins.

3. What is meant by "the graying of the American budget"?

4. How did Reaganomics impact government programs for the elderly?

Essay

1. Describe the health problems of the elderly, including those associated with a) physical health and b) mental health.

2. Discuss the stresses inherent in intergenerational caregiving.

3. Identify and describe four major value-related issues concerning the future direction of policy on programs for the elderly.

4. Discuss fully the concept of "continuum of care" for the elderly.

CHAPTER 11. SOCIAL WORK IN THE WORKPLACE

Chapter Outline

Resettlement Opportunity Services, Inc. (case study)
Social Work and Industry: A History
    The Middle Ages
    Industrial and Social Revolution
    Industrial Social Work in the Twentieth Century
The Forms of Industrial Social Work
Preparation for Practice with Employees and Employers
Value Conflicts for Social Workers in a Business Environment
Illustrations of Practice in Industrial Social Work
Research in Industrial Social Work
    Impact on Insurance Costs
    Approaches to Child Care
Human Diversity in the Workplace
Summary

Learning Objectives

After reading Chapter 11, the student should be able to:

1. Discuss the ways in which Jeanne West, in the case study, served the needs of Hmong refugees, especially the women clients.

2. Describe the uneven history of the social work profession's involvement in business and industry.

3. Describe five different forms of service delivery in occupational social work.

4. Identify the college courses that would be useful supplements to the social work major for students for students who wish to pursue careers in occupational social work.

5. Explain the value conflicts that are unique to social work practice in the workplace.

6. Define employee assistance programs.

7. Referring to the example in the text, discuss the potential impact a social work trainer can have in a state transportation department's EAP program.

8. Explain how research can be used to demonstrate the effectiveness and economic advantages to business of industrial social work programs.

9. Differentiate between affirmative action and equal employment opportunity programs.

10. Identify the 1978 U.S. Supreme Court case that established the basis for affirmative action hiring procedures.

Additional Reading Materials

Akabas, S. H., ed. "Social Work and the Workplace," Practice Digest Special Issue (1982).

Googins, B. Occupational Social Work: A Bibliography (Silver Spring, MD: National Association of Social Workers, 1987).

Masi, D. Human Services in Industry (Lexington, MA: D. C. Heath, 1982).

Teare, R. J. National Survey of Occupational Social Workers (Silver Spring, MD: National Association of Social Workers, 1987).

Tillema, R. G. "Starting Over in a New Land: Resettling a Refugee Family," Public Welfare 39(1981): 35-41.

Class Activities

1. Today most students have some type of employment experience. Form the class into several groups and ask each group, on the basis of its members work experiences, to develop a list of employment related needs that affect individuals, families, groups, corporations or businesses, and special populations, and that would be appropriately met by social work. Provide each group with paper and magic markers for listing their needs, and ask each to report their findings to the class.

2. Have your students research the availability of employment assistance programs wherever they or any members of their immediate family are employed and determine the eligibility requirements, the services provided, and the type of staff--including any social workers--involved in each case. Ask each student to report his or her findings to the class.

3. Invite your school personnel officer to speak to your class concerning school policies in the area of equal employment opportunity and affirmative action. If possible, ask him or her to provide class with copies of these policies.

4. Form the class into groups to identify and discuss the problems faced by new immigrants entering the United States' work force. Ask each group to identify specific ways in which social workers might intervene to help these immigrants and report its findings to the class.

TEST ITEMS

Multiple-Choice

a) 1. Resettlement Opportunity Services' primary role vis a vis the business community was:
a. advocating to obtain jobs for the agency's clients
b. counseling unemployed workers from refugee families
c. soliciting donations of goods and money for client families
d. monitoring compliance with federal and state employment regulations

c) 2. The primary service Jeanne West and her agency, Resettlement Opportunity Services, offered to the agency's clients was:
a. family counseling
b. financial assistance
c. assistance with their search for suitable employment
d. group therapy

d) 3. Among Southeast Asians, limited eye contact is a behavior intended to convey:
a. evasiveness
b. resistance
c. discomfort
d. respect

b) 4. The first known employee benefit programs were those established by:
a. General Electric and the Union Pacific Railroad in the 1930s
b. the organizations of craftspeople, artisans, and merchants known as "guilds" during the Middle Ages
c. the Scottish industrialist, Robert Owen, in the early 1800s
d. the H. J. Heinz Company of Pittsburgh in 1875

a) 5. The first occupational social workers were known as:
a. welfare secretaries
b. friendly visitors
c. human services managers
d. wobblies

c) 6. One of the first programs to offer a specialization in occupational social was that established:
a. at Smith College in the 1920s
b. at General Motors Institute in Flint, Michigan in 1935
c. at Columbia University in the early 1960s
d. at Brandeis University in 1976

d) 7. The historical development of occupational social work is best characterized as having been:
a. slow but steady
b. intense
c. carefully planned
d. uneven

b)   8. The primary purpose of most employee assistance programs is to:
     a. reduce employee absenteeism
     b. intervene whenever employee work performance suffers
     c. reduce employer health insurance costs
     d. assist employees with substance abuse problems

a)   9. The work ethic is a societal attitude that says:
     a. work is good and laziness is sinful
     b. quality of work is the single most important measure of employee performance
     c. the interests of the worker and the employer are identical
     d. a person's work determines her or his value

c) 10. Which of the following best describes the current status of occupational social work?
     a. it is in a state of decline
     b. it has recently become one of the largest fields of social work practice
     c. it is a rapidly growing field that is still evolving
     d. its future seems assured by recent federal legislation requiring all firms with over 50 employees to provide social work services to their staff

d) 11. Which of the following programs of study would not be recommended preparation for a baccalaureate level student interested in occupational social work:
     a. coursework and field placement in occupational social work at an accredited baccalaureate social work program
     b. a combined social work/business administration major
     c. a social work major with a business administration minor
     d. a major in personnel management with a minor in social work

a) 12. Value conflicts are most likely to arise for the social worker working in a business environment when:
     a. the quest for profit takes precedence over the welfare of people
     b. the social worker is a salaried employee
     c. the social worker is an outside contractor
     d. there is a conflict between government regulations and the employer's current policy

d) 13. Critics of occupational social work have argued that:
     a. business and industry is essentially exploitative
     b. social work cannot exist in a business environment without compromising its values
     c. the profit motive is essentially incompatible with a genuine concern for the welfare of employees
     d. all of the above

c) 14. One difficulty many managers have when dealing with employee problems is that they fail to recognize the symptoms of such problems. Another is:
     a. that they tend to act too harshly
     b. that they lack adequate training in personnel dismissal procedures
     c. that they often ignore the problem or defer action
     d. that they usually go directly to the employee rather than consulting a trained social work professional

b) 15. Referrals to an Employee Assistance Program (EAP) are usually classified as either:
   a. direct or indirect
   b. formal or informal
   c. public or private
   d. written or oral

a) 16. Current research on the effects of employee assistance programs on business insurance costs suggests that companies with such programs have:
   a. more claims but not higher insurance costs
   b. fewer claims but significantly higher insurance costs
   c. more claims and significantly higher insurance costs
   d. more claims but significantly lower insurance costs

d) 17. One service social workers can best provide to employers considering a child care program is:
   a. assistance with the recruitment and hiring of qualified staff
   b. advice about local regulations
   c. workshops for employees concerning alternatives to employer-sponsored child care
   d. information about the range of possibilities and help with the selection of an appropriate plan

c) 18. Equal employment opportunity may be best defined as:
   a. a policy that guarantees minorities will be considered for any position for which they apply
   b. a 1965 federal law that requires all firms above a specified size to hire a specified number of minority employees
   c. the right of all persons to work and advance on the basis of merit, ability, and potential
   d. the process of ensuring/guaranteeing that all persons have the right to work and advance on the basis of merit, ability, and potential

b) 19. Affirmative action may be best defined as:
   a. a policy that guarantees minorities will be considered for any position for which they apply
   b. the process of ensuring/guaranteeing that all persons have the right to work and advance on the basis of merit, ability, and potential
   c. the right of all persons to work and advance on the basis of merit, ability, and potential
   d. a 1965 federal law that requires all firms above a specified size to hire a specified number of minority employees

a) 20. In a 1989 case involving an action brought by white firefighters from Birmingham, Alabama, the U.S. Supreme Court ruled that:
   a. workers who believed they were adversely affected by affirmative action plans could file lawsuits alleging discrimination
   b. workers who believed they were adversely affected by affirmative actions could not file lawsuits alleging discrimination
   c. affirmative action programs are unconstitutional
   d. public agencies are not required to have affirmative action programs

77

T   1. The primary focus of Jeanne West's intake interview with new clients at Resettlement Opportunity Services was on employability.

F   2. Jeanne West believed that social workers must never become emotionally involved with their clients.

T   3. The Hmong women with whom Jeanne West worked were not permitted to meet with a male social worker or any male professional person unless accompanied by their husbands.

T   4. Work has come to define who we are and, to a considerable degree, how we feel about ourselves.

F   5. Most industrial workers in this country today are in control of their work environment and the destiny of their products.

T   6. The origins of the work ethic can be traced back to the Protestant Reformation.

T   7. The first recognized industrial social worker in the United States was, Aggie Dunn, who was hired by H. J. Heinz in 1875.

F   8. The Great Depression of the 1930s was accompanied by significant growth in the number of occupational social workers because of the increase in the human needs of the workforce.

T   9. The human relations movement of the 1930s and 1940s encouraged managers to adopt a more "person-centered orientation."

T   10. During the period from the close of World War II through the end of the 1950s, the social work profession appeared to lose interest in occupational social work.

F   11. Most employee assistance programs are staffed entirely by social workers.

F   12. There is, at present, only one basic model for the delivery of social services in the workplace.

T   13. Regardless of their initial training, occupational social workers should expect to enroll in continuing education programs and seminars throughout their career.

T   14. A generalist orientation is particularly appropriate for occupational social work because of the great diversity of responsibilities involved in such work.

T   15. Confidentiality is an area of special concern to both occupational social workers and employees.

F   16. Occupational social work is a field with relatively little potential for value conflict.

T   17. Employees who fail to comply with a formal referral to an employee assistance program will usually face job termination or other disciplinary action.

T   18. Social workers in employee assistance programs must sometimes be jacks-of-all-trades.

T   19. Case vignettes are a useful tool for social work trainers assigned to teach managers when and how to refer employees to an employee assistance program.

T   20. One important role of occupational social workers is to help employers meet federally mandated equal employment and affirmative action requirements.

Fill-In

1. (Affirmative action) procedures are designed to ensure that people who have traditionally been discriminated against have access to opportunities for employment, advancement, and admission to professional programs.

2. The social work ethic that requires social workers not to divulge information entrusted to them by clients is known as (confidentiality).

3. (Equal employment opportunity) programs are designed to ensure that equally qualified people will be considered for employment regardless of their race, ethnicity, gender, age, religion, or other personal characteristics.

4. The first occupational social workers were known as (welfare secretaries).

5. Like soldiers, survivors of accidents, personal assaults, rape, and other violence can suffer from serious emotional shock or pain known as (psychological trauma).

6. There has been a great increase in recent years in persons known as (the working poor) whose income is insufficient to meet their survival needs.

7. Another name for occupational social work is (industrial social work).

8. Fraternal organizations established during the Middle Ages by occupational groups such as craftspeople, artisans, and merchants to protect the interests of their members were known as (guilds).

9. Counseling programs provided by employers as a fringe benefit are known as (employee assistance programs).

10. Persons who seek the help of a social worker themselves are known as (self-referrals).

Short Essay

1. List at least three distinctive aspects of Hmong culture and discuss the impact of each on Jeanne West's work with her clients at Resettlement Opportunity Services, Inc.

2. Briefly describe the ways in which the industrial revolution altered the nature of work.

3. Identify and describe at least three of the five different ways in which occupational social work services may be delivered.

4. Briefly explain the reasons why some critics feel that social work and the business environment are incompatible.

5. Identify and provide examples of at least three of the "five A's" identified by Nancy Johnston and Irl Carter as the personal problems that most frequently cause employees to seek help from an employee assistance program or other professional source.

6. Briefly define and explain the differences between the concepts of equal employment opportunity and affirmative action.

Essay

1. Do you believe it is possible for a social worker to function effectively in a business environment? Why or why not?

2. Identify and describe the types of problems that are most frequently encountered in occupational and discuss their implications for an occupational social worker's pre-professional training and study.

3. Identify and describe the major costs and benefits (both financial and non-financial) of a typical employee assistance program. Then discuss at least one possible way by which each such cost and benefit might be measured for evaluation purposes.

CHAPTER 12.   THE FUTURE AND SOCIAL WORK

Chapter Outline

Trends in Current Social Work Practice
        Political Forces
        Economic Conditions
        Demographic Trends
        Technological Changes and Social Work
Career Tracks for Social Workers
        Selecting a Career in Social Work
        Social Work and Human Services
Employment Opportunities
Forecasting the Future
Summary

Learning Objectives

After reading Chapter 12, the student should be able to:

1. Discuss the outside political forces, economic conditions, demographic trends, and technological changes that are likely to influence the future of the profession of social work.

2. Give examples of social service programs that have undergone privatization.

3. Explain why the profession of social work must be especially attuned to women's issues and concerns.

4. Discuss changes that have taken place in the evolving American family.

5. Use the decision tree in Figure 12-2 to clarify or explain her or his selection of a career.

6. Differentiate social work and the human services.

7. Explain the career tracks available in social work, differentiating the professional from the preprofessional levels and noting where specific academic credentials are required to move from one level to the next.

8. Define the BACSW.

9. Discuss employment opportunities in social work as projected by the United States Department of Labor.

10. Refute the common belief that most social workers in the United States are employed by the government.

11. Using data from a recent national survey, describe current employment patterns for baccalaureate social workers in the United States.

Additional Reading Materials

Karger, H. J. and Stoesz, D. _American Social Welfare Policy: A Structural Approach_ (White Plains, NY: Longman, Inc., 1990).

Kleinkauf, C. _Social Workers and Politics: A Selected Annotated Bibliography_ (Anchorage: University of Alaska Press, 1986).

Linowes, D. F. "The Future of Privatization," _National Forum, The Phi Kappa Phi Journal_, Special Issue on Privatization (Spring 1990): 2-4.

Naisbett, J. _Megatrends_ (New York: Warner Books, 1988).

1990 Supplement to the Encyclopedia of Social Work (Silver Springs, MD: National Association of Social Workers, 1990).

Class Activities

1. Form the class into several groups and have each group plan the contents of an imagined "time capsule" reviewing the highlights of the social work profession in the 20th century. Explain, tongue in cheek, that the capsule is to be buried on the grounds of Hull House in Chicago and will be dug up and opened in the year 2060 on the 200th anniversary of Jane Addams' birth. Ask each group to select the 20 most important items (of manageable size and tangible form) they feel should be included in such a capsule. Then ask each of the groups to share their list of "social work artifacts" with the class.

2. Divide the class into two groups and provide each with a common list of issue areas. Ask one of the groups to prepare a 1996 platform covering these areas (and any others the group believes to be important) for the Republic Party, and the second group to do likewise for the Democratic Party. Then have each group report on the content of its platform.

3. Set aside a half day toward the end of the class for a social work job fair featuring potential employment opportunities within your local area. Insofar as possible, draw upon your student's knowledge of the local community to identify potential invitees and solicit student assistance with the logistics, publicity, and administrative tasks involved.

TEST ITEMS

Multiple-Choice

d) 1. Social work is best described as:
    a. a glamorous, high-status profession
    b. well understood by contemporary society
    c. immune to outside social and economic forces
    d. a profession with a distinctive set of values

a)   2. The increasing privatization of social services has been accompanied by:
     a. an increase in the number of "for profit" human service organizations
     b. an increase in federal funding for the housing of homeless families
     c. a reduction in federal defense spending
     d. a reduction in the fragmentation of social services

c)   3. Which of the following groups and organizations do <u>not</u> play a sig-
     nificant role in funding battered women's shelters?
     a. the United Way
     b. womens' social clubs
     c. the Office of Domestic Violence
     d. private individuals

b)   4. Underemployment is best defined as:
     a. the practice of hiring Australian workers
     b. employment at or near minimum wage
     c. the employment of minors under the legal working age
     d. a firms' failure to hire a sufficient number of workers

a)   5. Social workers often must choose the extent to which they will serve:
     a. as arms of the dominant institutional structures of our society or as
     agents of those who are excluded
     b. meals or provide clothing to the homeless
     c. as counselors or therapists to the mentally ill
     d. none of the above

d)   6. The three demographic trends that currently have the greatest impact on
     social work practice are:
     a. the increasing dominance of minority groups, rapid growth in the youth
     population, and the overall decline in population growth
     b. the continued growth of--the total U.S. population, the American Indian
     population, and "old old" segment of the population
     c. the growth of the "underclass," the emergence of women as a significant
     social force, and the decline in Hispanic and black political influence
     d. the "graying of America," the evolving structure of the American family,
     and the changing nature of the immigrant and refugee population

c)   7. The profession of social work is especially attuned to issues that
     concern women because:
     a. of the impending passage of the Equal Rights Amendment
     b. women now hold a majority of the administrative positions in social work
     c. it is comprised of significant numbers of women and serves a client
     population that includes many poor and vulnerable women
     d. the NASW Code of Ethics mandates such a concern

b)   8. Three types of technological advances that have had a particularly
     significant impact on social work practice in recent years are:
     a. industrial automation, computerization, and the rise of satellite
     broadcasting
     b. computerization, advances in communications, and advances in medical
     science
     c. advances in communications, advances in transportation, and the rise of
     bioethics
     d. advances in reproductive technology, computerization, and industrial
     automation

d) 9. According to the authors, the first question to ask yourself when
        considering a social work career is:
        a. How much can I expect to earn as a social worker?
        b. Am I comfortable working with people from cultural backgrounds other
        than my own?
        c. How do I want to work with people?
        d. Do I want to work with people?

a) 10. The terms "social work" and "human services":
        a. are often confused
        b. mean essentially the same thing
        c. both apply to any profession that works with people
        d. have no relationship to one another

b) 11. The notion of career tracks is based on the assumption that:
        a. different people should be able to pursue similar career objectives
        regardless of differences in their training
        b. it is possible to begin at a lower level on the career ladder and then
        move upward while progressing from one position to another
        c. the level at which one enters the profession determines one's career
        prospects
        d. each different area of practice is a self-contained whole

c) 12. NASW's Standards for the Classification of Social Work Practice divides
        all recognized categories of professional social work employment into two
        basic levels:
        a. voluntary and professional
        b. beginner and advanced
        c. professional and preprofessional
        d. introductory and professional

d) 13. Prior to 1965, the entry level of practice in social work required:
        a. a BSW degree
        b. certification by the Academy of Certified Social Workers
        c. a minimum of two years of field work
        d. an MSW degree

a) 14. The BACSW is:
        a. a certification plan for BSW's that parallels that of the ACSW for
        master's degree social workers
        b. the acronym for Bachelor of Arts Certificate in Social Work
        c. an advanced degree for BSW level social workers that involves one year
        of additional study at an accredited BSW level program
        d. a new requirement for entry level social workers

b) 15. The percentage of social workers who are employed in government
        settings is approximately:
        a. 19%
        b. 44%
        c. 83%
        d. 91%

c) 16. The largest single group of baccalaureate social workers are those employed:
    a. by the federal government
    b. in alcohol and drug abuse counseling
    c. in direct practice
    d. in occupational social work

d) 17. Employment of social workers through the year 2000 is expected to:
    a. gradually decline in all fields except alcohol and drug abuse
    b. remain approximately the same
    c. increase dramatically in all practice areas except with the aging
    d. increase faster than the average for all occupations

True-False

F 1. Social work as a profession is well understood by contemporary society.

T 2. Social workers are expected to work to make social institutions more humane and responsive to human needs.

T 3. In recent years, the federal government has increasingly looked to the private sector and local government as a source of funding for programs at the community level.

F 4. One consequence of the increasing fragmentation of social services has been a decline in case management.

T 5. In most communities today, only a small proportion of group homes are run by nonprofit organizations.

F 6. The Equal Rights Amendment was passed by Congress in 1972 and went into effect in June 1976 when Delaware became the 38th state to ratify.

T 7. It is estimated that persons 65 or older will comprise 13 percent of the U.S. population by the year 2000.

F 8. Single parent families now constitute a majority of all families with children in the United States.

T 9. Approximately 90% of all single parent families are headed by women.

T 10. Currently 500,000 people enter the United States each year through normal immigration procedures.

T 11. The 1986 Immigration Reform Act was primarily designed to control illegal immigration into the United States from Mexico and Central America.

F 12. Stringent government regulations ensure that the use of computerized databases in social work presents no risk to confidentiality.

T 13. Videotaping is widely used as a social work practice training tool.

T 14. One of the primary tasks of the social worker in a neonatal intensive care unit is to assess the child's home situation and provide the resources necessary to make it safe.

F   15. Social work's emphasis on the interactions between people and their environments is one it shares with virtually all other human-service professions.

T   16. One reason that the terms human services and social work are often confused is that human services is customarily defined in at least two different ways.

F   17. The 1981 NASW policy statement, "NASW Standards for the Classification of Social Work Practice," has today been replaced as the model for the classification of social work practice.

F   18. The two preprofessional level categories of social work practice are: social service aide and social service associate.

F   19. The four professional level categories of social work practice are: introductory professional, general professional, specialized professional, and advanced professional.

T   20. Only about 1.4% of social workers are employed by the federal government.

Fill-In

1. One stereotype that lingers on is that of the welfare worker dispensing ("the dole") to lazy, fraudulent recipients.

2. The coordinating and monitoring of all services provided to a client or family is known as (case management).

3. Most group homes in most communities today are owned and operated by (private corporations).

4. Since the mid-1970s, the private practice of social work has (expanded) significantly.

5. Women gained the right to vote in the United States in 1920 with the passage of (the Nineteenth Amendment).

6. On average, women in the United States can expect to outlive men by approximately (7.3 years).

7. Sheila Kamerman contends that it is the (function) rather than the structure of the nuclear family that has changed in recent years.

8. By 1985, (Asians) had become the fastest growing immigrant population in the United States.

9. There are approximately (8 million) applications for the 10,000 special immigration visas available annually through a lottery system.

10. In contrast to the "high tech" occupations, social work is sometimes said to be a "high (touch)" profession.

11. The hospital units where very low birth weight babies are normally cared for are known as (neonatal) intensive care units.

12. The decision tree presented in chapter 12 is designed to help with a choice of (career).

13. The academic requirement for the entry professional level of employment in is a (bachelor's) degree from an accredited social work program.

14. The highest level of social work employment is the (advanced) professional level.

15. The single most popular field of practice in recent years appears to have been (health care).

Short Essay

1. Identify the major political trends that affected social work practice during the past decade and discuss their consequences.

2. Identify and discuss at least two major changes in the American family that have affected social work practice in recent years.

3. List at least three ways in which computerization has affected social work practice.

4. Define the terms social work and human services and explain why they are frequently confused.

5. Identify and list the required credentials and experience for three of the four professional level social work employment categories.

Essay

1. What do you believe are the major political trends that will affect social work during the coming decade and what will be their impact?

2. Is the increasing privatization of social work services a beneficial or a detrimental trend? Why?

3. What impact is the increase in the proportion of persons 65 or older likely to have on social work practice and employment during the coming decade?

4. What impact has computerization had on the delivery of social services to date?

5. What, in your judgement, is the single most important practice-related question raised by advances in medical science to date?

6. Explain the primary difference between social work and each of the following human services professions: psychology, psychiatry, teaching, and the ministry.